I0024534

Edward Walsh

Irish popular Songs

Edward Walsh

Irish popular Songs

ISBN/EAN: 9783743330245

Manufactured in Europe, USA, Canada, Australia, Japa

Cover: Foto ©Thomas Meinert / pixelio.de

Manufactured and distributed by brebook publishing software
(www.brebook.com)

Edward Walsh

Irish popular Songs

IRISH POPULAR SONGS;

WITH

English Metrical Translations,

AND

INTRODUCTORY REMARKS AND NOTES.

BY

EDWARD WALSH.

Second Edition,

REVISED AND CORRECTED;

WITH

ORIGINAL LETTERS NEVER BEFORE PUBLISHED.

DUBLIN:

W. H. SMITH AND SON, ABBEY-STREET.

M. H. GILL AND SON, SACKVILLE-STREET.

AND ALL BOOKSELLERS.

DUBLIN :

PRINTED BY PETER ROE,

MABBOT-STREET.

TO

The People of Ireland,

AS A TRIBUTE TO THEIR MANY VIRTUES,

AND

WITH ARDENT ADMIRATION

OF

THEIR HIGH POETIC GENIUS,

AS EVIDENCED IN THEIR SONGS AND LEGENDS,

This Volume

IS INSCRIBED

BY

THEIR FRIEND AND COUNTRYMAN,

EDWARD WALSH.

PREFACE TO SECOND EDITION.

A T a time when efforts are being made to revive the use of the written language of our country, no apology is necessary for attempting to add our mite to the general fund, in the shape of a second and (so far as type, &c., are concerned) improved edition of the Irish words in native letters, with the translations and songs of the late Edward Walsh.

Music is to the Irishman what salt is to the Arab—it impresses his soul, it enters into his very being, and it is only the shame of exposing a weakness of his manhood that prevents his weeping when he hears some air of long ago—some plough tune whistled, that erst he heard when wandering over the familiar paths of his childhood—

" A stranger yet to pain."

Well we remember (though now forty years since) following Walsh in the twilight of an autumn evening, drinking in the odd chords that came from the little harp that lay on his left arm as he wandered, lonely and unknown, by the then desert Jones's-road, or reposed himself on one of the seats that at that time were outside the walls of Clonliffe House. It was then we first heard Casaḋ an t-Súgáin, "The Twisting of the Rope" —that beautiful air to which Moore adapted the no less beautiful words, "How dear to me the hour when Daylight dies!" We have ever known a difficulty in singing the words of the great poet to the air—there is none in Walsh's version; but then *it* is the pure vintage, and words and music come from the same source.

In our young days, in the remote lodges of Belmullet, away at Inver, and amongst the O'Donnells of that ilk who inhabited the almost unknown regions of Poulathomas, in wild Erris, we met many who could sing the native melodies, and give to the language that pathos which alone it is capable of receiving; but the march of intellect has only taught us to be ashamed of our nationality. The generous but indiscriminate supply of small harmoniums by the Board of National Education, and the Hullah System, have sent the music of poor Erin to the right-about; and you are much more likely now-a-days to hear "A che la Mórte," "La Malle des Indes," or "Li Biama" from Brindisi, than "Colleen das cruthan a Mbhow" or the "Coulin" echoing from the parlour of some comfortable shopkeeper of Killybegs or Westport, whose young ladies have just returned from school, where they learnt more of the phonograph than they did of "cut papers," and worked at hideous

attempts at illumination when they should have
been learning to make a shirt for their father, or
to diaper-darn their own stockings! The music
of their country was not to be thought of, and
shopkeepers' daughters who had perforce to speak
Irish in Berehaven, did not know a word of the
language when they came to fashionable Cork.

But a brighter day is dawning, and the publication of such songs as Walsh's must beget a taste
and raise Nationalism and Patriotism from the
low state to which they have fallen.

We have made no attempt to fix airs, or insti-
tute comparisons; we give the book as it came
from the author—there is nothing in it that
requires a justification or excuse. We believe it
to be a noble specimen of native genius, and as
such we offer it to our countrymen, confident in
their verdict, and strongly hoping to live to hear
the soul-stirring, heart-moving songs of the people
echoing in the vernacular through the verdant
groves of our NATIVE LAND.

J. S. S.

Dublin, June, 1883.

CONTENTS.

———oo———

viii   *Contents.*

INTRODUCTORY REMARKS

ON

IRISH POPULAR POETRY.

THE popular Songs and Ballads of Ireland are
as completely unknown to the great mass of
Irish readers, as if they were sung in the wilds of
Lapland, instead of the green valleys of their own
native land. These strains of the Irish Muse are
to be found in the tongue of the people only; and
while, for past centuries, every means had been
used to lead the classes which had partaken, even
in the slightest degree, of an English education,
into a total disuse of the mother tongue; when
the middle and upper ranks, aping the manners
of the English settlers located among them,
adopted a most unnational dislike to the language
of their fathers; when even in the courts of law
the sole use of the vernacular was a stumbling-
block in the way of him who sought for justice
within their precincts, and the youth who may
have acquired a smattering of education found it
necessary, upon emerging from his native glen
into the world, to hide, as closely as possible, all

knowledge of the tongue he had learned at his mother's breast; it is no wonder the peasantry should, at length, quit this last vestige of nationality, and assist the efforts of the hedge schoolmaster in its repression. The village teacher had long been endeavouring to check the circulation of the native tongue among the people, by establishing a complete system of espiery in these rustic seminaries, in which the youth of each hamlet were made to testify against those among them who uttered an Irish phrase. This will easily account for the very imperfect knowledge which the rising population of various districts have, at this hour, of the tongue which forms the sole mode of communication between their seniors. The poor peasant, seeing that education could be obtained through the use of English only, and that the employment of the native tongue was a strong bar to the acquirement of the favoured one, prohibited to his children the use of the despised language of his fathers. This transition was, and is still, productive of serious inconvenience to the young and the old of the same household in their mutual intercourse of sentiment. The writer of these remarks has been often painfully amused at witnessing the embarrassment of a family circle, where the parents, scarcely understanding a word of English, strove to converse with their children, who, awed by paternal command, and the dread of summary punishment at the hands of the pedagogue, were driven to essay a language of which the parents could scarcely comprehend a single word, and of which the poor children had too scant a stock to furnish forth a tithe of their exuberant thought.

Yet, in this despised, forsaken language are stored up the most varied and comprehensive powers for composition. Who that has heard the priest address his Irish-speaking congregation, and seen the strange power of his impassioned eloquence over the hearts of his hearers—how the strong man, the feeble senior, the gentle girl, were alternately fixed in mute astonishment, kindled into enthusiasm, or melted into tears, as the orator pourtrayed the mercies of heaven to fallen man— who that has witnessed this, and will not acknowledge its thrilling influence in the affecting simplicity of its pathos, and the energy of its bold sublimity? Who that has heard the peasant-mother lavish upon her infant these endearing expressions, which can hardly be conveyed in a comparatively cold English dress, and not call it the tongue of maternal tenderness? And I trust that he who can read the following songs in the original, will likewise confess that the Irish tongue can also express the most passionate ardour, the most sweetly querulous murmurings of love, and that rending grief which beats its breast upon the margin of despair.

It has been asserted that there is no language

better adapted to lyric poetry than the Irish. That
array of consonants which is retained in the words,
to show the derivation, and which appears so
formidable to the eye of an un-Irish reader, is cut
off by aspirates, and softens down into a pleasing
stream of liquid sounds, and the disposition of the
broad and the slender vowels gives a variety to
the ear by their ever-changing melody.

One striking characteristic in the flow of Irish
verse must principally claim our notice—namely,
the beautiful adaptation of the subject of the
words to the song measure—the particular em-
bodiment of thought requiring, it would seem, a
kindred current of music to float upon. Or, to
vary the figure, the particular tune so exquisitely
chosen by the Irish lyrist, seems the natural gait
of the subject, whatever that may be, from which
it cannot be forced, in a translation, without at
once destroying the graceful correspondence which
gives its most attractive grace to the original.

Miss Brooke has erred through her versions of
the " Reliques " in this respect, and so also, almost
generally, have the translators of Mr. Hardiman's
" Minstrelsy."

Another grace of the Irish language lies in the
number of its synonymes, which enables the poet
to repeat the same thought over and over without
tiring the ear. Its copiousness permits the raising
of a pyramid of words upon a single thought—
as, for instance, in the description of a beautiful

head of hair, the poet employs a variety of epithets, all of the same cognate race, yet each differing from the other by some slight shade of meaning. The rhymers of later times have carried this peculiarity in a blameable degree. In this species of composition, the translator is quite bewildered, and he seeks, in vain, for equivalent terms in the English tongue to express the graceful redundancies of the original!

In the sentimental and pastoral songs of Ireland, will be found those varied and gorgeous descriptions of female beauty and rural scenery, which have no parallel in the English tongue, and which, as men of learning have asserted, are equalled only in the rich and exuberant poetry of the East. In these Irish songs are to be found none of the indelicate and even gross allusions which so greatly disgrace the lyrical efforts of the best poets of England in the last century. Not but that Irish rhymers have often composed in the censurable manner to which we have alluded; but these reprehensible lays are to be found only in manuscripts, and are never sung by the people.

Some of these popular songs are genuine pastorals, possessing this pleasing feature, that while nothing fictitious blends with the strain, and the whole is perfectly true to nature, nothing coarse or vulgar is introduced, to displease the most refined ear, and all the beautiful and glorious objects of nature are pressed into the service of

the muse. The bloom of the bean-field is the
cheek of the rural nymph ; her eye, a freezing
star, or the crystal dew-drops on the grass at sun-
rise ; her sudden appearance, a sunburst through
a cloud of mist ; the majesty of her mien, the
grace of the white-breasted swan surveying his
arching neck in the mirror of the blue lake ; her
voice, the cooing of the dove, the magic sounds
of fairy music, or the speaking note of the cuckoo
when he bids the woods rejoice ; her hair
either ambery, golden, or flaxen—ringleted,
braided, perfumed, bepearled, sweeping the tie of
her sandal, or floating on the silken wing of the
breeze ! The enamoured poet will lead his love
over the green-topped hills of the South or West,
will show her ships and sails through the vistas
of the forest, as they seek their retreat by the
shore of the broad lake. They shall dine on the
venison of the hills, the trout of the lake, and the
honey of the hollow oak. Their couch shall be
the purple-blossomed heath, the soft moss of the
rock, or the green rushes strewn with creamy
agrimony, and the early call of the heath-cock
alone shall break their slumber of love !

Allegory was the favourite vehicle of conveying the political sentiment of Ireland in song, at
least since the days of Elizabeth. To this figure
the poets were inclined by the genius of the
tongue, as well as the necessity which urged to
clothe the aspirations for freedom in a figurative

dress. Erin, the goddess of the bard's worship, is a beautiful virgin, who has fallen within the grasp of the oppressor—all the terms of his tongue are expended in celebration of the charms of her person, her purity, her constancy, her present sufferings, her ancient glory! Her metaphorical names are many: the chief among that class are " Rós geal Dubh," " Graine Mhaol," " Droiman Donn;" or she sometimes appears invested with all the attributes in which the beautiful fairy mythology of the land enwraps the fabled beings of its creation. She leads the poet a devious route to many a rath and fairy palace, till at length, amid the shadowy forms of olden bards, and chiefs, and regal dames, and sceptred kings, she bids the wondering mortal proclaim to the Milesian Race that the period was at hand when her faithful friends would burst her bonds of slavery! The " Vision of John MacDonnell" is a beautiful instance of this species of composition, and is also very curious in illustration of the fairy topography of Ireland.

A few specimens to prove our remarks upon the power of Irish verse, may not, perhaps, be unacceptable to the reader. The following noble stanza is from a poem by Eoghan O'Rahilly, a poet of the last century, on a shipwreck which he witnessed on the coast of Kerry. The stanza and its translation are taken from O'Reilly's " Biography of Irish Writers ":—

Dob éagnaċ imirt na tuile re daor-ruaṫar
Méad na toinne re fuirneaḋ na gaoṫ guairnéin,
Taob na loinge 'sa fuirionn air treun-luasgaḋ,
Aig eiġeaḋ tuitim go grinniol gan dáil fuascailt;

The roaring flood resistless force display'd,
Each whirling blast the swelling surges sway'd,
The vessel burst—alas! the crew she bore
Scream'd in the deep, and sank to rise no more!

Donough MacNamara, a Waterford poet of the last century, in his mock Æneid, thus describes the roar of the Stygian ferryman as penetrating the remotest boundaries of creation:—

Do léig se gáir ós árd is béiceaċ,
Le fuaim a ġoṫa do ċriṫeadar na spéarṫaḋ,
Do ċualaḋ an ċruinne é 's ċuir ifrionn géim as!

He uttered an outcry and a roar—
At the sound of his voice the heavens were shaken,
All creation heard it, and hell rebellowed!

The following incentive to battle is from the pen of Andrew Magrath, called the *Mangaire Sugach*, another Munster poet:—

Sin agaib an t-am agus gabaig le na ċéile,
Preabaig le fonn agus planncaig meiṫ-ṗuic,
Leanaig an foġa ar ḋream an éitig,
'S ná h-ionntoiġeaḋ aen le sgáṫ ó'n-gleó!

The hour hath come—unite your force;
Rush with ardour, and strike the fat he-goats;

Follow up the assault on the perfidious race,
And let none swerve in terror from the conflict!

In "The Boat Song,"—one of the songs in the
present collection,—the poet thus apostrophises a
rock in Blacksod Bay:—

Ⱥ Ḋaoɨleɪn, a ċnoɪn-ċaɲɲaɪʒ ʒaɲḃ ʒan ɼʒáċ,
Ⱥɪɲ an ɲuaṫ-ḃaɲc-ɼo ɼúm-ɼa ḃɲeaċnɲʒ ṫo ɼáċ,
Ⱥn ċɲ̇ṁɪn leaċ, 'ɼ an ʒ-cuan-ɼo, ʒo ḃ-ɼaca ċú báṫ
Ʒan ċonċaḃaɪɲċ ċonn-ḃaɲɲa ʒeaɲɲaṫ maɲ ċáɪm!

O! Dilion, tempest-beaten rock, all rough and dark!
Look forth, and see beneath me now this bounding
    bark,
And say, if e'er thou boat beheld within this bay,
Wave mounted, cleaving, confident, like mine to-
    day!

The wind agitating the waters of the River
Funcheon is thus described by one MacAuliff, a
blacksmith of Glanmire, near Cork. I would beg
of the classical reader to compare this line with
that frequently quoted one in the first book of
Homer's Iliad:—

Ʒlɪonʒ-ʒoċaċ láɪtɪɲ a ʒ-caɪċɪoṁ na ṫ-ċonn.

Loud-clanging, forceful, wild-tossing the waves.

The following instance from the song of *Eadh
monn an Chnoic* will shew how the consonant
sounds are softened down by aspiration:—

Ʉ cḟil ɑlɲɲɲ ᴅeɑr ɲɑ b̄-ꝼɑɪɲɲeɑᴅɑ ʒ cɑꞃ,
Jr bꞃeɑʒ 'ʒuꞃ ꞃꞃ ʒlɑꞃ ᴅo ꞃḟile!

Maid of the wreathed ringlets, beautiful, exceedingly
    fair,
Blue and splendid are your eyes!

And again, in the same song as it is sung in the
South of Ireland:—

Ʉ cuꭑɑɪɲ ꞃɑ ꞃeᴅꞃc ɲɑċɑmꞃꞓɲe ꞃeɑl
Ꝼɑ ċoɪllꞇe ɑɪʒ ꞃꝑeɑlɑ ᴅꝑúċꞇɑ,
Ꝃɑꞃ ɑ b̄ꝼɑʒɑᴅꭑꞃꞓɲe bꞃeɑc 'ꞃꞃ loɲ ɑɪꝑ ɑ ɲeɑᴅ,
Ʉɲ ꝼɪɑᴅ 'ʒuꞃ ɑɲ ꝑoc ɑʒ bꞃꞇꝑe;
Ʉɲ ꞇéɲɪɲ ꞃꞃ bɪɲɲe ɑɪꝑ ʒéɑʒɑɪb̄ ɑʒ ꞃeɪɲɪꭑ,
Ʉɲ ċuɑɪċɪɲ ɑɪꝑ b̄ɑꝑꝑ ɑɲ úꝑ-ʒlɑɪꞃ,
Jr ʒo bꞃɑᴅ uɲ ċɪocꝼɑ ɑɲ b̄ɑꞃ ɑɪꝑ ɑꝑ ɲ-ʒoɪꝑe,
Ʉ lɑꝑ ɲɑ coɪlle cub̄ɑꝑċɑ!

My hope, my love, we will proceed
Into the woods, scattering the dews,
Where we will behold the salmon, and the ousel
    in its nest,
The deer and the roe-buck calling,
The sweetest bird on the branches warbling,
The cuckoo on the summit of the green hill;
And death shall never approach us
In the bosom of the fragrant wood!

In the allegorical song, *Rós geal Dubh,* the
poet's love for his unfortunate country, and his
utter despair of its freedom, are thus expressed:

Τá ʒμáḋ aʒaɱ aɱ láμ ḋμʒ
le blaʒaɪɲ aɲoɪr,
Ʒμáḋ cμáɪʒe, ʒμáḋ cáɾṁaμ,
Ʒμáḋ cjopaḋa,

Ʒμáḋ ḋ'ꝼáʒ ɱé ʒaɲ rláɪɲʒé,
Ʒaɲ μjaɲ, ʒaɲ μμʒ,
Jr ʒo bμaḋ, bμaḋ, ʒaɲ aoɲ ꝼaɪll aʒaɱ
Uɪμ Rór ʒeal Ḋuḃ!

My love sincere is centred here
This year and more—
Love, sadly vexing, love perplexing,
Love painful, sore,

Love, whose rigour hath crush'd my vigour,
Thrice hopeless love,
While fate doth sever me, ever, ever,
From *Rós geal Dubh !*

In the song of "Beautiful Deirdre," the following will illustrate what has been already said of
the power of the Irish in the use of synonymes :—

Jr caɱaμraḋ claoɲ, 'r ɪr cμaoḃaḋ, ċμaḋ-úμlaḋ,
Ʒaɪṫɲeaṁaḋ, ʒeuḋaḋ, ꝼaoɲ-ċar, ꝼeac-lúaɪɲeaḋ
leaḃaɪμ-ċeaμʒ, laoḃḋa, rlaoḋaḋ, rμaḋ-lúḃaḋ
U baċall-ꝼoɪlʒ ċaoṁ-ʒlaɲ ʒeuʒaḋ ꝼaḋ-ċúμraḋ.

Her ringlet-hair—
Curve-arching, meandering, spreading, curl-quivering,
Fascinating, stringlike, pliant-wreathing, restless-
swerving,
Free-extending, inclining, abundant, thick-twining,
Mildly-bright branchy, far-sweeping.

The next is a proof of the exquisite feeling of
the elegiac muse of our valleys. A lover is weeping over the grave of his betrothed :—

Nuaiṗ iṙ ᴅóiʒ le ṁo ṁ̇ηηᴛiṗ ʒo ιη-bjṁ-ṙe aiṗ ṁo
    leaba,
Аiṗ ᴅo ċuaṁba ṙeaᴅ ḃj'ṁ ṙiηᴛe ó oṙᴅċe ʒo ṁaiᴅ-
    iη,
Аʒ cuṗ ṙjoṙ ṁo ċṗuaᴅᴛaiη, iṙ aʒ cṗuaᴅ-ʒol ʒo
    ᴅaiηʒioη,
Ƈṗé ṁo ċaιljη cιṙ̇η ṙᴛ̇uaṁaiᴅ, ᴅo luaᴅaʒ ljoṁ ηa
    leaηḃ !

When the folk of my household suppose I am sleep-
    ing,
On your cold grave till morning the lone watch I'm
    keeping ;
My grief to the night wind for the mild maid to
    render,
Who was my betrothed since infancy tender !

I shall conclude these quotations with this
simile, taken from one of the songs in the present
collection :—

Cḃoηaiṗc ṁé aʒ ᴛeaċᴛ ċuʒaṁ j ᴛηe láṗ aη ᴛ-ṙléιḃe,
    А)aṗ ṗéιlᴛjoη ᴛṗjᴅ aη ʒ-ceó !

I saw her approach me along the mountain,
    Like a star through a mist !

I shall now introduce to the reader's notice
some of the poets of the last century, from whose

writings many of the songs in this collection are taken. Some of these songs belong to an earlier period. *Rôs geal Dubh*, for instance, is supposed to have been composed in the time of Queen Elizabeth; but the names of the writers of some of the best in the collection are now unknown. In these songs, the historian or moral philosopher may trace the peculiar character of our people; and from fragmented phrases and detached expressions, ascertain the " form and pressure " of the times to which they belong, even as the geologist bears away fragments of old world wonders, whence to deduce a theory or establish a truth. He will trace the ardent temper and un-broken spirit of our people in these undefined aspirations for freedom—the allegorical poems; their vehement and fiery love, chastened and sub-dued beneath the yoke of reason, by deep religious feeling, in their pastoral songs; and in the elegiac strains he will trace the intense feelings that exist in the Irish heart, as the mourner pours his despair over the grave of departed beauty, or sighs, on the margin of a foreign shore, for one green spot in his own loved island which he can never more behold.

These song writers are, doubtless, the lineal descendants of the bards of preceding centuries. Their poems, however, are not works of art; they are, with few exceptions, the efforts of untutored nature—the spontaneous produce of a rich poetic soil. But if these wild lyrics thrill with electric power to the heart, what must be the effect of the finished productions of that happier period when the chiefs of the land protected the craft of the minstrel!

Chief among these poets, as distinguished for his-extensive learning and bardic powers, stands John MacDonnell, surnamed Claragh, a native of Charleville, in the County Cork. He was the contemporary and friend of John Toomey, a Limerick poet, celebrated for his convivial temper and sparkling wit. The "Vision," of MacDonnell, with some other pieces, come within the present collection. He was a violent Jacobite, and his poems are chiefly of that character. In his time, the poets held "bardic sessions" at stated intervals, for the exercise of their genius. The people of the districts bordering upon the town of Charleville yet retain curious traditions of these literary contests, in which the candidates for admission were obliged to furnish extempore proofs of poetical ability. O'Halloran, in his "Introduction to the History of Ireland," makes honourable mention of this gifted man, and says that he was engaged in writing a history of Ireland in the native tongue. MacDonnell made also a proposal to some gentleman of the County Clare to translate Homer's Iliad into Irish. "From the specimen he gave," says O'Halloran, "it would seem that this prince of poets would appear as respectable in a Gathelian as in a Greek dress."

MacDonnell died in 1754, and was interred near Charleville. His friend and brother poet, John Toomey, wrote his elegy, which may be found in Mr. Hardiman's "Minstrelsy."

Andrew Magrath, surnamed the *Mangaire Sugach*, from whose writings I have largely extracted, was a native of the County Limerick. He practised, for a considerable time, the business of a pedlar, or travelling merchant, an occupation that gave occasion to the designation, *Mangaire Sugach*, which denotes the *Jolly Merchant*. His poems are very numerous, and greatly varied, being chiefly satirical, amatory, and political. This man possessed a genius of the highest order. His humorous pieces abound with the most delicate touches, for, as his occupation of pedlar led him into all grades of society, his discrimination of character was consequently very acute. His love songs are full of pathos, and, so far as I have been able to observe, entirely free from the taint of licentiousness. He, however, lived a vicious, sensual life, and by his irregularities incurred the censures of the Roman Catholic priesthood. It was on occasion of his being refused admittance into the Protestant communion, after his expulsion from the Catholic Church, that he wrote his "Lament," where the portraiture of his strange distress leaves the reader at a loss whether to weep at his misfortune, or laugh at the ludicrous expression of his sorrow.

Owen O'Sullivan, usually named *Eoghan Ruadh*, or *Owen the Red*, from the colour of his hair, was a native of the County Kerry. He lived at a somewhat later period than either MacDonnell or Magrath, and was also, like Magrath, a very eccentric character. O'Sullivan sometimes followed the employment of an itinerant labourer, in which occupation he would make periodical excursions into the Counties of Cork, Limerick, and Tipperary, during the reaping and potato-digging seasons. In the summer months, he would open a hedge school in the centre of a populous district, where the boys of the surrounding hamlets, and the " poor scholars " who usually followed in the wake of Owen's perambulations, were taught to render the Greek of Homer and the usual school range of Latin authors into Irish and English. I should observe that Owen the Red wrote and spoke the English tongue with considerable fluency. Many of his satires, written in that language, against the Volunteers of '82, are yet preserved in the neighbourhood of Churchtown and Charleville, in the County of Cork.

O'Sullivan's productions are satirical, elegiac, amatory and political. He is the favourite poet of the Munster peasantry, and their appreciation of the potato-digging bard does high credit to their critical discrimination. His strain was bold, vigorous, passionate, and feeling; his only fault being a redundancy of language to which he was led by the inclination of the Irish tongue, and his own vehemence of temper. He died in 1784.

The following extract from the life of Owen O'Sullivan, as I have given it in the "Jacobite Reliques," will furnish a glimpse of this unfortunate genius :—

"There are doubtless many of my readers who now hear of Owen Roe O'Sullivan for the first time. To them, perhaps, it will be necessary to say, that Owen Roe was to Ireland what Robert Burns, at a somewhat later day, was to Scotland—the glory and shame of his native land. I know no two characters in my range of observation that so closely resemble each other as Burns and Owen Roe. The same poetical temperament—the same desire of notoriety—the same ardent sighings for woman's love—the same embracing friendship for the human family—and the same fatal yearnings after "cheerful tankards foaming," alike distinguished the heaven-taught minstrels. Like Burns, Owen Roe first tuned his reed to the charms of nature and the joys of woman's love—like Burns, the irregularity of his life obliged the clergymen of his persuasion to denounce him; and, like him, he lashed the priestly order without ruth or remorse—like Burns, he tried the pathetic, the sublime, the humorous, and, like him, succeeded in all. Nor does the parallel end here; they were both born in an humble cottage; both toiled through life at the spade and plough; and both fell, in the bloom of manhood, in the pride of intellect, the victims of uncontrolled passion!"

William Hefferan, more usually called *Uilliam Dall*, or *Blind William*, a native of Shronehill, in the County Tipperary, was contemporary with MacDonnell and Toomey, with whom he often tried his poetic powers in the literary battles of the bardic sessions. He was born blind, and spent the greater part of his life, a poor houseless wanderer, subsisting upon the bounty of others. His pieces are political, elegiac, and amatory. The tenderness of his amatory muse is refined and sweet in the highest degree. His allegorical poem, *Cliona of the Rock*, says Mr. Hardiman, "would in itself be sufficient to rescue his memory from oblivion, and stamp him with the name of poet. The machinery of this ode has been a favourite form of composition with our later bards. They delighted in decorating these visionary beings with all charms of celestial beauty, and in this respect, our author appears to have been no mean proficient. His description is heightened with all the glow and warmth of the richest oriental colouring, and the sentiments and language are every way worthy of the subject."

His *Caitlin ni Uallachán* and other pieces, in this collection, will furnish a fair specimen of his abilities.

Another poet of this century was Donough Roe MacNamara, a native of Waterford, who, finding that the profits of his hedge school, in which he taught Greek and Latin to the peasantry, were inadequate to his support, resolved to try his fortune as a labourer in Newfoundland. He embarked; but on the second day of the voyage, the vessel in which he sailed was chased back upon the Irish coast by a French privateer, and poor MacNamara once more took to the teaching trade. At the suggestion of a Mr. Power, he afterwards wrote a metrical account of his adventure. In this poem he sets out with a description of his poverty—the manner in which the whole parish contributed to fit him out—the fascination of his landlady and her fair daughter, in Waterford— a storm at sea—sea-sickness of the passengers—a vision in which the queen of the fairies takes him to the realm of departed spirits, where he beholds the shades of Irish warriors, and hears strange political revelations, &c., &c. This mock Æneid contains passages of extraordinary power, and rare flights of humour. MacNamara also produced many political and amatory songs.

The foregoing are the writers from whose works I have chosen some of the pieces in this collection. Contemporary poets, of whose poems I have not availed myself are Eoghan Ó'Rahilly, a native of Kerry, a man of learning and great natural abilities. The peasantry of the bordering Counties of Cork, Limerick, and Kerry, yet recite his poems, and cherish the memory of his caustic wit and exquisite humour. O'Halloran makes honourable mention of this poet. Denis and Connor O'Sullivan, brothers, authors of many excellent political and amatory songs, were also natives of Kerry. In the same district, at a somewhat later period, lived Fineen O'Scannell, a man of high poetical merit, the author of many poems. Edmund Wall was also a satirical poet of much celebrity in the County of Cork.

The Reverend William English, a friar of the City of Cork, was a poet, highly facetious and satirical. Timothy O'Sullivan usually named *Teige Gaelach*, a native of the County Waterford, was also a poet of great celebrity. His works are numerous, consisting of odes, elegies, political songs, and pastorals. His elegy on the death of Denis MacCarthy, of Ballea, in the County Cork, is a beautiful specimen of this species of composition. In early life his conduct was very irregular, and many of his poems licentious ; but in after time he became sincerely penitent, and devoted his talents to the composition of sacred poems and hymns, many of which have been collected and published under the title of " Timothy O'Sullivan's Pious Miscellany."

In this passing view of the writers of the last century, I have confined myself to those of the South of Ireland alone. Even many of these I must pass over in silence, and shall close with some account of John Collins, whose genius and learning eminently qualify him to stand among the first of modern writers in Ireland. Collins taught school at Skibbereen, in the County Cork, where he died, in 1816. His poems are held in high estimation; his best production, or perhaps the best in the modern Irish, being his poem on "Timoleague Abbey." Collins has given an Irish translation of Campbell's "Exile of Erin," which admirably proves, if proof were necessary, the power of the Irish language. None will pronounce this translation in any instance inferior to the celebrated original, while, in many passages, the Irish version rises far superior in harmony of numbers and feeling of expression!

In conclusion, I beg leave to say a word or two respecting the songs in this collection. I have admitted nothing among them calculated, in a moral or political point of view, to give offence. I have also been careful to avoid that error which I already censured in others—namely, the fault of not suiting the measure of the translation to the exact song-tune of the original. The Irish scholar will perceive that I have embodied the meaning and spirit of each Irish stanza within the compass of the same number of lines, each for each; and that I have also preserved, in many of the songs, the cæsural and demi-cæsural rhymes, the use of which produces such harmonious effect in Irish verse. I offer these songs to the public as evidence of the poetic spirit of our people. To the reader who cannot peruse the original, I have to say, that the English versions are faithful, and, in most instances, perfectly literal transcripts of the Irish; and that our hills and valleys, and milking bawns, and every cottager's fireside, are vocal with hundreds of songs, which want but the aid of a poet, himself one of the people, speaking their tongue, and familiar with its idioms, to recommend them to public notice in an English dress.

It is fit to state that I have copied into this little work some of the songs which Mr. Hardiman has left untranslated in the "Minstrelsy," and also that I have selected from manuscripts some songs which I subsequently found had been already used by Mr. Hardiman. Some of my versions, however, are different from his.

In consequence of the neglected state of the Irish language during the last two centuries, considerable irregularity has arisen among writers in the use of its orthography. This will be apparent to anyone who considers what the fate of a language must be, which, ceasing to be the vehicle of learned instruction, descends to the use of men unskilled in the rules of composition, and ignorant even of the modes of inflecting nouns, or conjugating verbs. The songs in this collection, I am proud to say, are as free as possible from grammatical error, Mr. Owen Connellan,

Irish Historiographer to their late Majesties, George IV. and William IV., translator of the " Annals of the Four Masters," and author of a " Grammar of the Irish Language," &c., having kindly undertaken to read the Irish throughout, and to correct every apparent error of the text.

E. WALSH.

Dublin, January, 1847.

Edward Walsh was interred in the Mathew Cemetery, Cork, where a Celtic Cross bears the following inscription, in Irish and English:—

eaobáro breacnac,
an file agur an fir Cinionnac,
o'éag an reireaó lá oo ñí,
lugñára m.o.cccl.
San mbliaóain ceacracaó
agur cúig oa aoir.
Do tógbaó an Cnor hag ro
Man leacc-Cuimne oo le a
Cairoib agur le lucc
ag a raib móinñear air.
Jo o-cugaió Dia ruamñear
Siorr'uibe o'a anam.

EDWARD WALSH,

The Poet and Translator,

Died August 6th, 1850,

Aged 45 Years.

Erected to his Memory

By a few Admirers of the Patriot and the Bard.

God rest his Soul.

The following more correct rendering of the Irish has been furnished to us by a friend:—

EDWARD WALSH,

The Poet and True Irishman,

Who Died the 6th August, 1850,

In the 45th year of his age.

This Memorial Cross was erected in memory of him by his Friends and by the People, who esteemed him much.

May God give eternal rest to his Soul.

WALSH'S IRISH POPULAR SONGS.

——:o·——

20 Essex Quay, Dublin,
24th March, 1883.

SIR,

From amongst many of Edward Walsh's letters in my posses-
sion, I send you four which I have selected for insertion in your
new edition of his "Irish Popular Songs."

These letters are most characteristic of the meekness of the poor
fellow in the dark hours of his homeless adversity ; in them are to
be found traces of the poetic, patriotic, and most tender domestic
feeling as well as a spirit of christian resignation and humility
under a load of undeserved punishment,

Poor Walsh ! with great talents and goodness of heart, his life
experiences in his own dear Isle were anything but pleasurable.

As you aided him in putting his first edition through the press, I
don't wonder at your being so anxious to make this edition an
interesting and successful one.

With best wishes for the realization of your hopes in connection
with the re-issue of Walsh's " Irish Popular Songs."

Yours,

PATRICK TRAYNOR.

To Mr. Peter Roe.

ORIGINAL LETTERS OF EDWARD WALSH.

Duke's-row, Summer-hill,
Dublin, January 2nd, 1844.

DEAR SIR,

I did not receive your letter till late last night, though left
here yesterday morning.

I called at Machen's at 10 to-day. He informed me that the
printer did not yet give him your second number, and that many
gentlemen called to enquire for it, and seemed disappointed. I
called at the residence of a barrister of note in the city—after-

B

wards one of those fiery spirits who are carrying out the present movement of freedom,—and he told me that he likewise called at Machen's for the songs. He begged . of me to leave him my metrical version of the songs to show to his friends. He has a high opinion of my abilities, and says that my aid in giving an elegant translation would be powerful in recommending them to many English readers. He says it would be a good plan to introduce your literal version with the Irish—that is, to give the prose English under the Irish, word for word, without regard to the arrangement—for the use of them who would study the tongue, and they would be many. He says such songs would take well. He has given me some business in the way of writing.

The artist I spoke of informs me that Curry says the last line of the *Creevin Erin* in your song is not belonging to that song at all ; and I am clearly of opinion that it does not suit the measure of the other lines. Curry remarks that the two first lines are from a long song, the others are from a Jacobite song, and the last taken from some other song.

I have to say that it strikes me if the songs were got up in a clever way, they would succeed.

You will scarcely be able to read this, which I write in a confounded hurry.

Yours faithfully,

E. WALSH.

P.S.—I have no certain knowledge when I leave town, or whether I go at all—I'll know in a week. The *Creevin Erin* is in the mouth of all the clever fellows here.

----

23 Duke's-row, Summer-hill,

Dublin, January 5th, 1844.

Dear Sir,

I got your letter this morning, and have great pleasure in now replying to that favour.

I called into Machen's at half-past 2 o'clock yesterday, and up to that time the printer did not send him your songs.

I did not go to hear Mr. S——'s lecture at the Rotundo. I did not know that you were acquainted with him. I now suppose him to be the person of whom we were speaking, and whose brother I knew.

I was in the hope that the board would allow me back to my snug residence at Tourin, but they decided against it yesterday, though Sir R. M—— and the superintendent applied in my behalf. I am grieved that my poor wife and infants will be disturbed in their calm solitude, and sent up here in winter weather—*God pardon the doers of this injustice.* You will say, perhaps that it is the best course for my future advancement. It may be so, but I am not well fitted for the bustle of a town life, and besides, I dread if my health, which is not very robust, should fail—I dread the fate of my family; but I must now bear the charge and pray to God to assist me.

With regard to our projects respecting the songs, I understand you to say that you will bear all the expenses of printing, paper, &c., and after deducting all costs from the sales, you then at the end of six months will equally share the net profits remaining, with me. If this should be so, I am content. I'll engage to give you spirited translations,—talent is my only stock-in-trade, and I'll be no miser of it. In all other respects, Mr. Daly, reckon me as one who would die rather than lie or deceive.

I would wish, when you give the metrical version of the songs, that you gave the name of the translator. Mr. Lane recommends me not to forget this, as it might procure me notice.

That Mr. Curry sent the artist I was speaking of to me last night, to say that he would wish to know me. I am now about to go to him to the Academy, and shall enquire at Machen's about the songs. It still strikes me the last line of the *Creevin* has not the same measure nor number of feet with the other lines. Try, Mr. Daly. I shall with great pleasure try my hand at your songs, Nos. 2 and 3, if you send up the Irish and your literal version. I wish you were here, and then we would pull *harmoniously* together. I am very lonely and sad away from my own beloved wife and children, and cannot well settle down to anything till they come; I have written for them.

Believe me, with all truth, dear Mr. Daly,
Yours very faithfully,
E. WALSH.

23 Duke's-row, Summer-hill,
Dublin, Wednesday, January 10th, 1844.

DEAR SIR,

I have thrown out no hint of your dealing unfairly by me, but I understood from you both " by word and write," as Burns says, that I was to share half *the profits.* That you meant so if I paid half the expenses as they occurred, I do not now doubt, because you tell me so, but I did not understand it so before. However, I am willing to *sing* for the thing you mention, that is one-third, as I cannot get more unless I contribute to the outlay. Are you satisfied, Mr. Daly?

I am prepared at all times to try my rhyming powers, though the *vis poetica* will not rush forth at my call at all times; however, never ask me if I am prepared, but always send without ceremony; send the Irish and the literal version. What you translated *link* in the *Creevin* I could not for some time understand the meaning of. I've learned it means a " *ringlet of hair;*" you should render it ringlet— it is highly poetical; your translation bore me from the meaning. I have written to Mrs. Walsh, and mentioned you. When she calls (if she travels by that way), provide her some decent safe lodging house to sleep in; she is anxious to see " Edward," and I don't think she will linger on the road. Your civil and kind invitation pleases me, Mr. Daly.

I was greatly pleased with your intention of giving the interlinear version according to my first suggestion. If you gave it without regard to the grammatical order of the English, but word for word in the Irish, it would be of service to my poetic version, by turning the reader from instituting comparisons between your accurate version and my looser one.

I called to-day at Machen's. He tells me the songs are taking right cleverly, but he complains of the manner in which the second number is got up. It is not fit for a street ballad, in type and paper. The letterpress and paper would damn the best work of the day. I told him you were taking it out of the printer's hands altogether, and he seemed pleased. 'I bought your first number, and am greatly pleased with its cleverness, and also at its respectable appearance.

I earnestly beg of you, unless you wish to ruin *the Irish character of the work*, not to print your *Irish* in either the Roman or Italian character.

The old Irish type is the type of their nationality ; alter that, and *you destroy it.* These are my own suggestions. I have not spoken yet to anyone on the subject, but shall, perhaps, with Mr. Duffy tomorrow. You will pardon me, and attribute to my present situation the manner in which I send your communication.

I beg to remain yours,

E. WALSH.

P.S.—I am confident Mr. C. G. Duffy will agree with me in saying that the Irish should be done in Irish types.

Richmond Cottages, Summer-hill,
Dublin, March 7th, 1844.

Dear Sir,

I trust you will pardon me for not replying earlier to your letters, when I assure you that I have so lengthened my hours of labour, that I scarcely have time to say my prayers, which, as a good Catholic, you are aware I am bound to do at least twice a-day. I thank you for the newspaper, which I now return. The notice was good, and a very keen logical critic to whom I showed it, upon reading the song, said it was in every way equal to " Craovin Aowen." I beg you will send me all the papers you may get containing critical notices of our work, and I shall faithfully return them. I took care on Tuesday or Wednesday last (I don't remember which) to write to Mr. Duffy, at Rathmines, mentioning the honourable testimony which the songs elicited from the provincial Press, and your regret and disappointment the *Nation* —the powerful leader of public opinion—should not honour you with a single remark. I accompanied this with a request that he would give us a favourable notice on Saturday's *Nation.* But Mr. Duffy neither gave the requested notice—as you must already have perceived,—nor sent me a private line in answer to my communication. This neglect on Mr. Duffy's part fills me with surprise, and I would assuredly have had a personal interview with him to ascertain the cause, had I time sufficient to visit him. This is an unnatural state of society, where a man having no pretension to literary merit, is so chained down to the galley oar of exertion for what heaven allots to the wild beast of the hill—his " daily bread,"—that he has not only no time to think of God and his glorious kingdom come—to listen to the communing of heaven's angels with his own immortal spirit,—but cannot spare an hour from his task-time to cross a town or a street upon a common errand of business ! But so it is.

I called at Goodwin's, but the proof was not ready. They told me that they would forward you one on Saturday, and that I could have another at six o'clock on Saturday night, but the severe storm of that evening blew the memory of Goodwin and Co. and all his proof sheets clean from my *cranium*, as I passed along in the sweeping strife of the elements.

I never perceived my cleverness at entering fully into the true spirit of Irish song till I read D'Alton's translation. I have many stanzas of the translated songs, evidently improved upon the old bard, and have scarcely ever fell much beneath him in conveying the wrongs and feelings of our race. A portion of this is because I am intimately acquainted with the manners and feelings of the people, and feel, indignantly feel, myself with all a poet's feeling, the curse and crime of the tyrant. You were scarcely out of town when a friend informed me that you made a very profitable hit by the sale of some Irish works; this rejoiced me exceedingly, though I would be better pleased to hear it otherwise than at second-hand, but I am delighted to hear it at any hand. You will believe this when, in addition to my own assertion, I assure you that a certain friend of mine who is a deep phrenologist, says, upon an examination of my skull, that I have " Benevolence and Attachment " uncommonly developed.

I expected Owen Roe, my favourite poet, before this. I am impatient to see how his English suit will fit him. Heaven speed the literary taylor.

E. WALSH.

IRISH POPULAR SONGS.

DÁNTA DÚTĊASAĊ NA H-ÉIRIONN.

STUAIRÍN NA M-BAĊALL M-BREAĠ RÉIĊ.

I.

Táiḋ na peulta 'na reараḋ air an aeḋar,
An ġrian a'r an ġealaċ na luiḋe,
Tá an ḟairge tráiġte ġan braon,
'S níl péim aġ an eala mar bioḋ ;
Tá an ċuaiċín, a m-barraḋaiḃ na n-ġéuġ,
Ḋ'á ḟíor-ráḋ ġur éalaiġ rí uainn,
A rtúairín na m-baċall m-breáġ réiḋ
Ḋ'ḟáġ Éire faoi ḟaḋṫṛṛi cruaiḋ !

II.

Trí níḋ ḋo ċíḋim tréiġ an n-ġráḋ,
An peacaḋ, an bár, a'r an ṗian,
Aġur m'inntín ḋá ínrin, ġaċ lá ḋaṁ,
M'aiġne ġur ċráḋ rí le ciaċ—
A ṁaiġḋean, ḋo ṁill tú a'm lár mé,
Aġur m' impíḋe ó'm láiṁ ċúġatra n-iar,
Mo leiġear ó na raiġioḋaiḃri a'm lár,
'S ġo b-faġaiḋ tú na ġrára ó Ḋhia !

IRISH POPULAR SONGS.

THE MAID OF THE FINE FLOWING HAIR.

I.

The sun hath gone down in the sky,
　The stars cease their heavenly way,
The tides of the ocean are dry,
　The swan on the lake hath no sway;
The cuckoo but adds to our care,
　Who sings from his green, leafy throne,
How the maid of the fine flowing hair
　Left Erin in sadness to moan!

II.

Three evils accompany love,
　These evils are Sin, Death and Pain—
And well doth each passing hour prove
　Thou'st woven around me their chain!
Oh, maiden that woundedst me sore,
　Receive this petition from me,
And heal my fierce pain, I implore,
　So GOD yield his mercy to thee!

III.

Jr bịnne ị 'ná aŋ beịⱦⱡịŋŋ 'ⱬ ná 'ŋ lⱨⱨⱬ,
'S ŋa ceịleaḃaⱬ ŋa cćéịⱬⱬeaċ ⱬá cịaⱬⱬ ;
Jr ⱦealⱬaịⱦe ị 'ná aŋ ⱦéuⱬ ⱬⱬéⱬ aŋ ŋ-ⱦⱬⱨċⱬ,
'S ịⱬ ⱦịoⱬ-ⱦeaⱬ ȝaċ alⱬ aŋŋ a clịaḃ ;
Ⱬa pịoḃ ⱬaⱬ aŋ eala aịⱬ aŋ ⱬⱬⱬáịȝ,
'S ⱦⱦịȝ lịoⱬ ȝuⱬ ḃⱬeaȝa ị ná'ŋ ȝⱬịaŋ ;
'S é ⱬo ċuⱬⱬaịⱦ ȝéuⱬ ⱬaⱬ ⱬuȝ ⱬé ⱦị ȝⱬáⱦ,
'S ȝo ⱬ-ⱦeáⱬⱬ lịoⱬ ŋaċ ḃ-ⱦeịcⱬịŋŋ ị ⱬịaⱬ !

—:o:—

CⱰSⱰḞ ⱰN Ⱬ-SUȝⱰJN.*

I.

Naċ é aŋ caⱬ ⱬaⱬḃ ċaⱬ aŋŋ ŋa h-áịⱬeⱬị ⱬé,
'S a lịaċⱬ caịlịŋ ⱦeaⱬ ⱦo ⱦáȝaⱬⱬa ⱬo ⱦịaịȝ ;
Ⱬáŋịc ⱬịe ⱬⱬeaċ 'ⱬ aŋ ⱬeaċ ⱬaịḃ ȝⱬáⱦ ȝeal ⱬo
ċléịḃ,
'S ċⱨⱬ aŋ ċaịlleaċ aⱬaċ aịⱬ ċaⱬaⱦ aŋ ⱬ-ⱬⱨȝáịŋ
ⱬé !

---

* This is said to be the original song composed to that delightful
tune, " The Twisting of the Rope." Tradition thus speaks of its
origin.   A Connaught harper having once put up at the residence
of a rich farmer, began to pay such attentions to the young woman
of the house, as greatly displeased her mother, who instantly con-
ceived a plan for the summary ejectment of the minstrel.   She pro-
vided some hay, and requested the harper to twist the rope which

III.

Her voice doth the viol surpass,
   Or blackbird's sweet notes on the tree,
More radiant than dew-sprinkled grass,
   In figure and feature she be:
Her neck like the swan's on the wave,
   Her eye hath a light like the sun ;
And oh, that my lost heart I gave,
   Or saw her who left me undone!

——:o:——

THE TWISTING OF THE ROPE.

I.

What mortal conflict drove me here to roam,
Though many a maid I've left behind at home ;
Forth from the house where dwelt my heart's dear
   hope,
I was turned by the hag at the twisting of the rope !

she set about making. As the work progressed and the rope
lengthened, the harper, of course, retired backward, till he went
beyond the door of the dwelling, when the crafty matron suddenly
shut the door in his face, and then threw his harp out of the window.
The version sung in the south of Ireland has some additional
stanzas, but I give the song as it is found in Hardiman's
" Minstrelsy," vol. i., where it is left untranslated.

II.

Ꝿá bꞃꞌꝺeann ꞇu lꞁom, bꞁꝺ lꞁom ꝺo ló a'ꞅ ꝺ'oꞁꝺce ;
Ꝿá bꞃꞌꝺeann ꞇu lꞁom, bꞁꝺ lꞁom óꞅ comaꞁꞃ an
ꞇ-ꞅaoꝣaꞁl ;
Ꝿá bꞃꞌꝺeann ꞇu lꞁom, bꞁꝺ lꞁom ꝣaċ óꞃꝺlaċ ann ꝺo
ċꞃoꞁꝺe ;
'S é má leuꞃ naċ lꞁom ꞇꞃaꞇꞃóna ꞇú maꞃ mꞃaoꞁ !

III.

Aꞅ ꞅꞌoꞅ a Slꞁꝣeaċ ċꞃꞃ mé eóluꞅ aꞁꞃ mo ꝣꞃáꝺ,
Aꞅ ꞅuaꞅ a ꞃ-Ꝣaꞁllꞁb ꝺ'ól mé léꞁ mo ꞅáꞇ ;
Ꝺaꞃ bꞃꞁꝣ mo baꞃa muꞃa léꞁꝣꞃꞁꝺ ꝺamꞃa maꞃ a ꞇáꞁm
Ꝺéanꞃaꞁꝺ mé cleaꞅ a baꞁꞃꞃeaꞅ ꞅꞁubal aꞅ na mꞃáꞁb !

——:o:——

ꝰAꞁꞀꞁꞓAꞒꝶ ꝣꞓAꞀ AꞂ ꞀAꞓ.

I.

Ꝿaꞁꝺꞁꞃ mꞁoċ ꝺo ꝣabaꞅ amaċ
Aꞁꞃ bꞃuaċ loċa Léꞁꞃ,*
An ꞅamꞃaꝺ aꝣ ꞇeaċꝺ, 'ꞅan ċꞃaob ꞃe ꞃ'aꞁꞅ,
'Ꝣuꞅ loꞃꞃꞃaꝺ ꞇeꞁꞇ ó'ꞃ ꞃ-ꝣꞃéꞁꞃ,
Aꞁꞃ ꞇaꞁꞅꝺꞁol ꝺam ꞇꞃe baꞁlꞇe-pꞃꞃꝺ,
'Ꝣuꞅ bánꞇaꝺ mꞁꞃe, ꞃéꞁꝺ,
Cꞁa ꝣeabaꞁꞃ le'm aꞁꞅ aċ cꞃꞁꞁoꞃ ꝺeaꞅ,
le ꝰaꞁꞃeaꝺ ꝣeal aꞃ lae.

* *Locha Lein, Loch Lene*, the Lake of Killarney, in Kerry.

II.

If thou be mine, be mine both day and night,
If thou be mine, be mine in all men's sight,
If thou be mine, be mine o'er all beside—
And oh, that thou wert now my wedded bride!

III.

In Sligo first I did my love behold,
In Galway town I spent with her my gold—
But by this hand, if thus they me pursue,
I'll teach these dames to dance a measure new!

——:o:——

THE DAWNING OF THE DAY.

I.

At early dawn I once had been
    Where Lene's blue waters flow,
When summer bid the groves be green,
    The lamp of light to glow—
As on by bower, and town, and tower,
    And wide-spread fields I stray,
I meet a maid in the greenwood shade,
    At the dawning of the day.

II.

Ní raib rtocaið na bróg, cóir, ná clóca,
  Aɲ mo rtóɲ ó'n rpéɲ,
Act folt fionn óɲóa ríor ʒo tɲoiʒ
  Aʒ fár ʒo báɲɲ an féɲ;
Bɾð calán cɲɾ́ðte aice 'na ʒlaic,
  'S aɲ ðɲɾ́úct ba ðear a rʒéiɾ,
Čuʒ baɲɲ-ʒean ó ðenur ðear,
  Le fáiɲeað ʒeal aɲ lae!

III.

Sɾ̃ð aɲ bɾɾʒðeać ríor le'ɲ air
  Aɲ bɾɲɲre ʒlar ðo'n b-feuɲ
A maʒað léi bjor ðá ɾɲ̃ɲðeaɾ̃ ʒo pɲar
  Waɲ mɲaoi nać rʒaɲfaɲ léi
A ðubaɲt rí ljom na bɲɾr mo ćljú
  Sʒaoil mé aɲ rɾubal, a ɲéic,
Sɲ iað a n-ðear na roɾllre aʒ teaćð
  Le fáiɲeað ʒeal aɲ lae!

——:o:——

BEAN ÐUB AN ʒLEANNA.

I.

A bfacað tú ɲó an ccúala tú
  Aɲ rtuaɲɲe ðob' áille ʒɲaoi,
A' n-ʒleaɲ̃ta ðuba, 'r mé aɲɲ uaiʒɲior,
  ʒan ruaiɾ̃ɲior ðo ló na ð'oɾðć'—
Béiljɲ caoɲ aɲ t-ruaɲ-ɲoirʒ
  Ðo buaɲ mé 'r ðo bɲeðóaiʒ mo ćɲoɾðe;

II.

Her feet and beauteous head were bare,
   No mantle fair she wore,
But down her waist fell golden hair
   That swept the tall grass o'er ;
With milking-pail she sought the vale,
   And bright her charms' display,
Outshining far the morning star,
   At the dawning of the day !

III.

Beside me sat that maid divine,
   Where grassy banks outspread—
" Oh, let me call thee ever mine,
   Dear maid," I sportive said.
" False man, for shame, why bring me blame ?"
   She cried, and burst away—
The sun's first light pursued her flight,
   At the dawning of the day !

——:o:——

THE DARK MAID OF THE VALLEY.

I.

Oh, have you seen my fair one,
   The brightest maid of beauty's train,
Who left me thus deploring,
   In deep, dark vales, my love-sick pain—
That mild-ey'd, sweet-tongu'd maiden,
   Who left a wounded heart to me,

Ꝋo beaṅnaċꞇ ᚠéin ᵹo buan léi,
Ꝣa ꝺꞇi aɲ ccuaɲ úꝺ bé áiꞇ a' ɱ-bꞃö!

II.

Aꞇá ᚱé ᚱᵹꞃiobꞇa a b-pꞃionɲꞇa
Ꝺo ċoɱ ᚱeaɲᵹ 'ᚱ ꝺo ɱala ċael,
Iᚱ ꝺo béilin ꞇaɲɲö ᚠaoi ᚱiɲ
Na ᚱaoilᚠiɲɲ ꝺo ᗸéaɲᚠaꝺ bꞃéaᵹ;
Ꝺo ċꞃob aᚱ ᵹile ɱine
Ioɲɲa aɲ'ᚱioꝺa 'ᚱ ná cluɱ ɲa ɲ-éaɲ,
Aᚱ buaꞃꞇa cꞃáiꞇe biɱ-ᚱe
Nuaᚱ ᚱɱaoiɲiɱ aiꞃ ᚱᵹaꞃúiɲɲ léi!

III.

Aɲ uaiꞃ ᗸeaꞃcaᚱ í, ꝺo ċéiᵹ ɱé,
Le ᵹéuꞃ ᚠeaꞃc ꝺa ᵹɲaoi 'ᚱ ꝺa ᚱɲó,
A ɱioɲa cioċa ᵹléᵹeal,
A ꝺéaꝺ ꝺeaᚱ, 'ᚱa ꝺlaoiꞇ-ᚠolꞇ óiꞃ;
Ba ᵹile a ꝺꞃeaċ ná Ꝺéiꞃꝺꞃe*
Cꞃɲ laoċꞃaiꝺ ɲa Aᚌiꝺe aiꞃ ᚠeöꝺ,
'S ɲa Bláɲaꝺ ɱiɲ ɲa ᵹ-claeɲ-ꞃoᚱᵹ,
Le aꞃ ꞇꞃaoċaꝺ ɲa ɱilꞇe ꞇꞃeöɲ.†

* It is said that Deirdre was confined, from the period of her birth, in a fort or tower, by Connor, King of Ulster, because a druid had foretold she would cause great calamity in the kingdom. When she grew up to womanhood, Naois, with his two brothers, bore off the beautiful captive to Scotland, when the king of that country, smitten by the fatal charms of the lady, formed a plan to destroy her lover. They were thus forced to flee from Scotland, and Connor, hearing of their distress, allured them over to Ireland, by promises of pardon, where the three brothers were slain by his order. For this deed of perfidy, Connor, abandoned by his nobles, saw Ulster ravaged from shore to shore, and bathed in the blood of its bravest warriors! See Keating's " Ireland," Haliday's edition, page 371.

My blessing I bequeath her,
  Where'er the gentle maiden be!

II.

Rare artists have engraven
  Her slender waist, her beauteous brow,
Her lip with sweetness laden,
  That once I thought would truth avow;
Her hand than down far fairer,
  More sleek than silk from India's shore;
And oh! in grief I'm pining,
  To think I've lost her evermore!

III.

With love my heart was glowing,
  When first I spied the lovely fair,
With breast of snowy fairness,
  And white teeth, and golden hair—
She shone more bright than Deirdre,
  The curse of Meathean chiefs of pride,
Or mild-ey'd beauteous Blanit,
  By whom a thousand heroes died!

† Blanit was daughter of the king of the Isle of Man. When the Red Branch Knights plundered that island, this lady, who, it is said, surpassed in beauty all the women of her time, was adjudged to Curaigh MacDaire. Cuchullin claimed her as his prize, but he was overcome by Curaigh in single combat. Sometime after, Cuchullin with a large body of men, attacked and slew Curaigh in his palace. Blanit then departed with Cuchullin into Ulster. Thither did the bard of Curaigh follow her; and one day finding Connor, Cuchullin, and Blanit at the promotory of Ceann Beara, he instantly clasped her within his arms, as she stood on the edge of a steep rock, and flinging himself downward, they were both instantly dashed to pieces!—See Keating's "History of Ireland," Haliday's edition, page 405; and also, "Transactions of the Gaelic Society."

IV.

Ꙃ plúp ꞃa m-baꞃ, ꞃa τꞃéʒ mé
    Ꙃꞃ baeτlaċ le ꞃaꞃτ ꝺá ꞃτóꞃ,
Ꙃaꞃ ċlꞃú, ʒaꞃ ṁeaꞃ, ʒaꞃ béaꞃa,
    Ꙃċꝺ bleaꝺáꞃaċτ ꞃꞃ bꞃꞃꝺeaꞃ ꞃꞃ ʒleó ;
Iꞃ bꞃꞃ ꝺo ꞃꞃꞃꞃꞃꞃꞃ ꝺꞃéaċτa
    Bꞃeaʒa Ꙃaoꞃꝺeꞃlʒe ꝺꞃꞃτ oꞃꝺċe aꞃ ꞃóʒṁaꞃꞃ,
'S ꝺo ꞃʒꞃꞃobꞃꞃꞃꞃ ꞃꝺaꞃꞃ ꞃa Ꞝéꞃꞃꞃe,
    Ꙃo léꞃꞃ-ċeaꞃτ, 'ꞃ ꞃa mꞃꞃleaꝺ móꞃ !

——:o:——

SEOLꙆꝜ NꙆ N-ꙄꙆꙎNꙆꝜ.

I.

Lá ꝺa ꞃabaꞃ aꞃꞃ ċaoḃ aꞃ ʒleaꞃꞃa,
    'S mé aʒ ꞃeólaꝺ ꞃa ꞃ-ʒaṁaꞃ ꞃá'ꞃ bꞃáꞃaċ,
Caꞃaꝺ oꞃꞃ ꞃꞃéꞃꞃ-ḃeaꞃ ṁaoꞃꝺa, ṁaꞃꞃeaṁꞃꞃl,
    Cꞃꞃꞃ, τaꞃꞃ, baꞃaṁaꞃl, ꞃáꞃꞃeaċ ;
Ꝺ'ꞃꞃaꞃꞃaꞃʒeaꞃ ꞃéꞃꞃ ꝺoꞃ ꞃꞃéꞃꞃ-ḃeaꞃ ċaꞃlce,
    Ꙃ ꝺ-τꞃocꞃaꝺ ꞃeal am ꞃáꞃꞃτꞃʒeaċꝺ,
'S lé ꞃáꞃꞃeaꝺ aꞃ lae beaꝺ 'm aꞃaoꞃ ꞃoꞃaꞃ ꞃeaꞃaꞃꞃ
    Ꙃʒ ꞃeólaꝺ ꞃa ꞃ-ʒaṁꞃaꝺ ꞃá'ꞃ b-ꞃáꞃaċ!

II.

Ꙃτá cꞃaꞃꞃ cuḃaꞃτa a lꞃꞃb ꞃa coꞃlle,
    'S τꞃʒꞃom aꞃaoꞃ ʒo lá ꞃaoꞃ,
Béꞃꝺ ceól ꞃa ꞃéuꞃ ꝺaꞃ ʒ-cuꞃ ċum coꝺla,
    'S ꝺꞃꞃlle ꞃꞃ τoꞃaꝺ a ꞃáꞃ aꞃꞃ :
Ꙃ ꞃꞃéꞃꞃ-ḃeaꞃ ṁoꝺaṁꞃl ꞃa bꞃoꝺ oꞃτ maꞃꞃʒ,
    'S é ċleaċꝺamaꞃ 'ꞃ áꞃ ꞃꞃáꞃꞃoꞃꝺe ;
'S aʒ ꞃmτeaċꝺ uaꞃꞃ ꞃéꞃꞃ ꝺꞃꞃτ aꞃꞃ maꞃꝺꞃꞃ,
    Ꙃeabaꞃꞃ póʒ aꞃ baꞃꞃa mo láꞃꞃ uaꞃꞃ!*

* The literal meaning of this line is : "you will receive a kiss from me from out of the top of my hand." It shows that the custom

IV.

Fair flower of maids, resign not
  My faithful heart for senseless boor,
Who rich in worldly treasure,
  In all my glorious gifts is poor—
I who, in Autumn evening,
  Can bid the Gaelic song resound,
Or sing the olden glory
  Of Fenian chiefs and kings renown'd!

——:o:——

LEADING THE CALVES.

I.

One evening mild, in summer weather,
  My calves in the wild wood tending,
I saw a maid, in whom together,
  All beauty's charms were blending—
" Permit our flocks to mix," I said,
  " 'Tis what a maiden mild would,
And when the shades of night are fled,
  We'll lead our calves from the wild wood."

II.

" There grows a tree in the wild wood's breast,
  We'll stay till morn beneath it,
Where songs of birds invite to rest,
  And leaves and flowers enwreath it—
Mild, modest maid, 'tis not amiss ;
  'Twas thus we met in childhood ;
To thee at morn my hand I'll kiss,
  And lead the calves through the wild wood !"

of kissing hands in salutation has prevailed among the Irish
peasantry.

III.

Aʒ ꞃeólaᵭ na n-ʒaṁna ᵭ'ꝼáʒ me 'n baɩle,
'S ceann nɩ bꝼaʒaᵭ ʒo lá ᵭɩoḃ,
Aꞇa m'aꞇaɩꞃ ʒan céɩll am ᵭɩaɩʒ ꞃan m-baɩle,
   A'ꞃ mo ṁáꞇaɩꞃín buaᵭanꞇa cꞃáɩꞇe;
Ʒeaḃam ceaᵭ ꞃaon ó ṁaon na coɩlle,
   Ꝼeuꞃ ᵭo ꞇaḃaɩꞃꞇ ʒo lá ᵭóɩḃ,
'S le ꝼáɩneaᵭ 'n lae béaᵭ 'm aꞃaon 'naꞃ ꞃeaꞃaṁ,
   Aʒ ꞃeólaᵭ na n-ʒaṁna ꝼá'n b-ꝼáꞃaċ.

——:o:——

COꞂꝂAꞀ Óʒ.

I.

Ꞇáɩᵭ na coɩlm aʒ ꞃúʒꞃaᵭ, 'ꞃ an ꞃaṁꞃaᵭ aʒ ꞇeaċꞇ,
'S an bláꞇ aʒ bꞃɩꞃeaᵭ ꞇꞃé ṁullaċ na ʒ-cꞃann amaċ,
Aꞃ ꞇoɩnn ꞇá'n bɩolaꞃ ʒo ꞇꞃɩopallaċ, ʒlíṁeaċ, ʒlaꞃ,
'S na coꞃcóʒa aʒ ꞃɩleaᵭ le h-ɩomaᵭ ᵭe ꞃuʒaᵭ na
   m-beaċ.

II.

Iꞃ ɩomᵭa ꞇoꞃꞇa a'ꞃ meaꞃ aɩꞃ an ʒ-coɩll ꞃo ꞃuaꞃ,
A'ꞃ óɩʒ-ḃean ṁaɩꞃeaċ ċeaꞃꞇ an ꞇ-ꞃeanʒ-ċoɩꞃp
   ꞃuaɩꞃc,
Ceuᵭ bó baɩnne, capall ʒꞃoɩᵭe, 'ʒuꞃ úaɩꞃ,
Coɩꞃ laoɩ* na m-bꞃeac, nɩo ċꞃeaċ mé aɩꞃ ᵭɩbɩꞃꞇ
   uaɩꞇ!

---

* The River Lee, which rises at Gougane Barra, and dividing as it approaches Cork, washes that city on its north and south sides,

III.

" With calves I sought the pastures wild ;
　　They've stray'd beyond my keeping—
At home my father calls his child,
　　And my dear mother 's weeping—
The forester, if here they stray,
　　Perhaps in friendship mild, would
Permit our stay till the dawn of day,
　　When we'll lead our calves from the wild wood."

——:o:——

CORMAC OGE.

I.

The pigeons coo—the spring 's approaching now,
The bloom is bursting on the leafy bough ;
The cresses green o'er streams are clustering low,
And honey-hives with sweets abundant flow.

II.

Rich are the fruits the hazly woods display—
A slender virgin, virtuous, fair, and gay ;
With steeds and sheep, of kine a many score,
By trout-stor'd Lee whose banks we'll see no more !

and, again uniting, forms that beautiful estuary, the harbour of
Cork. Spenser speaks of
　　" The spreading Lee that, like an island fair,
　　Encloseth Cork with its divided flood."

III.

Táit na h-éin ag déanaḋ guṫa agus ceóil,
Táit na laoiġ ag géimneaḋ go treun cum roċair
na m-bó;
Táit na h-éirg ag neubaḋ corraḋ air an b-feóir,
Ar mir féin a'm aonar a'r Cormac óg!

——:o:——

AIR BARR NA G-CNOC 'S AN IME G-CEIN.*

Seáġan Mac Doṁnaill, ccт.

I.

Seal do ḃjora am ṁaiġdjon féiṁ,
Jr anoir am baintreaċ caiте ṫréiṫ;
Tá mo ċéile a treabaḋ na d-тonn go tréan,
    Do ḃárr na g-cnoc 'r an ime g-céin.

Crir fá.

'Sé mo roġa é do ṫoġar do'm féin,
Jr maiṫ an doṁṅin go d-таḃanfunġ é,
Air ron a ḃeiṫ air bórd a long gan baoġal,
    Do ḃarr na g-cnoc 'r an ime g-céin!

II.

Jr go b-feiceadra an lá, a rтóр mo ċléiḃ,
M-béiḋ na clig da m-búallaḋ, ir na drumaiде
da léir,
Do ġall тrompa ag gaḃáil gaċ áiтrioṁ réiḋ,
    Do ḃárr na g-cnoc 'r an ime g-céin!
Crir fá.
'Sé mo roġa é do ṫoġar, 7c.

---

* This song is said to be the first Jacobite effort attempted by
MacDonnell. If this be so, the prince whose exile he deplores is

III.

The little birds pour music's sweetest notes,
The calves for milk distend their bleating throats;
Above the weirs the silver salmon leap,
While Cormac Oge and I all lonely weep!

——:o:——

OVER THE HILLS AND FAR AWAY.

I.

Once I bloom'd a maiden young,
A widow's woe now moves my tongue;
My true love's barque ploughs ocean's spray,
    Over the hills and far away.

CHORUS.

Oh! had I worlds, I'd yield them now,
To place me on his tall barque's prow,
Who was my choice through childhood's day,
    Over the hills and far away!

II.

Oh! may we yet our lov'd one meet,
With joy-bells' chime and wild drums' beat;
While summoning war-trump sounds dismay,
    Over the hills and far away!
Oh! had I worlds, &c.

James, the son of the deposed monarch, James II., in whose favour
the Scotch revolted in the year 1715.

III.

Jr ʒo ḃ-ḟeịceaḋra conóịn aịn rтóп mo ċleịḃ,
Ḋo ṫóʒḟaḋ ceó aʒur bnóṅ ḋo ʒaoḋaịl,
Ʒaċ Ḃíʒ aтá anra ḋoṁaṅ ḋá ṁéịꙍ
Aʒ úṁlaċт ḋó le coṅịnaḋ Ḋé.
          Cꙟn ḟa.
'Sé mo noʒa é ḋo ṫoʒaꙏ, 7c.

IV.

Ʒnáḋ mo ċnoịḋere aṅ Pnịoṅnꙏ aṅ Réx,
Sé rịúꙍ aṅ péálтa ʒṅịḋeaṅ ḋṅṅ тeaꙏ,
Ʒuꙏ bịṅne lịom ná ceól na ṅ-éaṅ,
Ḋo ḃaпn na ʒ-cnoc 'ꙏ aṅ ịme ʒ-céịn,
          Cꙟn ḟa.
'Sé mo noʒa é ḋo ṫoʒaꙏ, 7c.

V.

Sꙟʒḟeaḋ rịoꙏ aịn ċnoc ʒo ḣ-áпꙍ,
Jr ʒeaḃaꙍ ó Homer cleịте aṁ láịṁ,
Ma ʒeịḃịm тoịl ʒo rʒпịoḃaꙍ mo ꙏáịṫ,
Aịn ʒṅịoṁaптa rꙟlт ịr maịṫ mo ʒпáḋ.

          Cꙟn ḟa.

'Sé mo noʒa é ḋo ṫoḃaꙏ ḋom ḟéịn,
Jr maịṫ aṅ ḋoṁꙟṅ ḋ-тaḃaпꙏꙟṅ é,
Cuṅ a ḃeịṫ aịn bóпꙍ a lonʒ ʒaṅ ḃaoʒal,
Ḋo ḃaпn na ʒ-cnoc 'ꙏ aṅ ịme ʒ-céịn!

III.

Oh ! that my hero had his throne,
That Erin's cloud of care were flown,
That proudest prince would own his sway,
      Over the hills and far away !
   Oh ! had I worlds, &c.

IV.

My bosom's love, that prince afar,
Our king, our joy, our orient star ;
More sweet his voice than wild bird's lay,
      Over the hills and far away !
   Oh ! had I worlds, &c.

V.

A high, green hill I'll quickly climb,
And tune my harp to song sublime,
And chant his praise the live-long day,
      Over the hills and far away !

CHORUS.

Oh ! had I worlds, I'd yield them now,
To place me on his tall barque's prow,
Who was my choice through childhood's day,
      Over the hills and far away !

ᴍᴜɪʀɴɪɴ ɴᴀ ᴊʀᴜᴀɪᴊᴇ ʙᴀɪɴᴇ.*

I.

2l m-baɪle ɴa h-ɪɴʀeᵗ ʀɪaɴ,
2l ᴄá mo ᴊɴáʊ le blɪaʊaɪɴ,
Jɾ áɪlɴe í 'ɴa ᴊɴɪaɴ aɴ ᴄ-ʀaṁɴa—
'S ᴊo ʙ-ʀáʀaɴɴ mɪl 'ɴa ᴏɪaɪʊ,
2lɪɴ loɴᴊ a coʀ ʀaɴ ᴄ-ʀlɪaʙ,
Ⅎá ʀuaɪɴe aɴ uaɪɴ ᴄaʀéɪʀ ɴa Saṁɴa—
Ⅎo ᴊeaʙaɪɴɴ ᴊaɴ ʀᴄaʊ mo ċɪall,
Ⅎa ɴ-ᴊaʙaɪɴɴ í am lɪoɴ,
2lʀ ċɴɴʀɪɴɴʀe aɴ bʀóɴ-ʀo ʊɪom ᴊaɴ ʙuaɪʊʀeaʊ.
2lɪɴ ċoṁaɪɴle ɴuᴊaʊ ɴɪaṁ
Nɪ ʀóʀʀaʊ aċᴄ mo ṁɪaɴ,
Sɪ 2lɴɴɴɪɴ ɴa ᴊɴúaɪᴊe báɪɴe.

II.

2lᴊ ᴏɴoɪċeaʊ ɴa h-aɪʙɴe móɪɴe‡
Ċoɴaɪɴceaʀ mo ʀᴄóɴaċ,
2lɪɴɴʀɪɴ ʊeaʀ ɴa ɴ-óɴ-ʀolᴄ ʙ-ʀáɪɴɴeaċ,
'S ᴊo m-ba ṁɪlʀe ᴊo ʀaʊa a ʀóᴊ,
Ná mɪl 'ʀ ɴá ʀɪúcʀaʊ aɪɴ bóɴʊ,
'S ɴá ʊeaᴊ-ʙlaʀ ʀoᴊaɪl ʀɪoɴ Spáɪɴɴeaċ.
2l ʊá ċɪoċ ċoɴɴa cʀɴɴɴ,
Báɴ, ṁɪlɪʀ, cuṁɴa, bʀeáᴊ,

---

* This beautiful song is preserved in Hardimau's "Minstrelsy," vol. i., but is left there untranslated.

† Literally, *the Town of the Island*—Ballinahinch, in the County of Galway, where was founded, in 1356, a monastery of Carmelite friars. On a small island in the lake of Ballinahinch are the ruins

BELOVED OF THE FLAXEN TRESSES.

I.

At the *Town of the Isle,* my dear
Abides this long, long year,
Than the summer sun more brightly shining;
Where'er her footsteps go,
Fair honey-flowers will grow,
Even though 'twere winter's dark declining!
If to my net she sped,
'Twould ease my heart and head,
Where cruel love his burning brand impresses;
For all that living be,
I'll choose no mate but thee,
Beloved of the flaxen tresses!

II.

At the bridge of the Avonmore,
I saw my bosom's store,
The maiden of the ringlets yellow—
More sweet her kisses be
Than honey from the tree,
Or festive Spanish wine, of flavour mellow!
Her bosom, globes of white,
Sweet, fragrant, perfect, bright,

of a castle erected in the time of Elizabeth.   A river runs from the lake into Roundstone Bay.

‡ The Owenmore, a river of the County Mayo, flowing into Blacksod Bay.

ⅦⱰⱹ ṙneaċⱦa bⱦaⱦ ⱦá ċáⱹⱹaⱦ aⱹⱹ ṙléⱦbⱦⱦb ;
'S ⱬo ⱹ-ⱬoⱹⱹeaⱹⱹ aⱹ ċuaċ ⱬaċ aⱳ,
Ⰰ láⱹ aⱹ ⱬeⱹⱳⱹⱦⱦ ⱦall,
'S a ⱳ-baⱦle ⱳ-bⱦⱦeaⱹⱹ ⱳo ⱬⱹáⱦ ⱦ'á bⱹéaⱬaⱦ.

Ⅲ.

Ⰶá ƀ-ⱱaⱬaⱹⱹ-ⱱe ⱳo ⱹoⱬa
Ⰶe ⱳⱹáⱦƀ ⱦeaⱹa aⱹ ⱦoⱦⱹaⱹⱹ,
Ⰰⱬuⱱ ⱱáⱬaⱦⱳ oⱹⱹⱦa ⱹoⱬaⱹⱹ ⱱáⱹⱦa,
'S ⱹéⱦⱹ, ⱳaⱹ a ⱦeⱦⱹ ⱹa leabaⱦⱹ,
Ⱦa'ⱹ ċⱹaéb aⱦcⱦ óⱱ a ⱬ-cⱦoⱹⱹ,
'S ⱦáⱦⱦ ⱹá ceuⱦⱦa ⱱeaⱹ ⱬo ⱦúbaċ a ⱹ-ⱬⱹáⱦ léⱦ.
'S é ⱱaⱳaⱦl-ⱱeo ⱦo ⱳolaⱦ
Leⱦⱱ aⱹ ⱬ-céuⱦ ⱹⱦⱬ Solaⱦⱹ,
'S ⱦⱱ aⱦcⱦ ⱱo ⱦá aⱹ ⱹoⱱc ⱦⱱ áⱦlⱹe ;
Ⱃéⱦⱦⱦⱬⱦ ⱳo ⱦoċaⱹ,
'Ⱬuⱱ ⱱaeⱹ ⱳé o báⱱ obaⱹⱹ,
Ⰰ Ⰰⱦⱬⱹⱹⱦⱹ ⱹa ⱬⱹúaⱦⱬe báⱦⱹe.

——:o:——

Ⰰⱹ ⰓOS ⰃⰽⰰL ⰂⰟBⱦ.*

Ⅰ.

Ⱦⱱ ⱱaⱦⱦa aⱹ ⱹéⱦⱹ ⱦo ⱦuⱬ ⱳe ⱱéⱹⱹ
O'ⱹⱦé ⱬo ⱹⱦú,
Ⰰⱹ ⱦoⱳall ⱱléⱦb aⱳⱦⱬ, ⱬo ⱨ-ⱦⱹealⱦa, éaⱦⱦⱹoⱳ,
Ⱳaⱹ a b'eolaċ lⱦóⱳ,

---

* *Rós geal dubh, the white-skinned, black-haired Rose,* is one of
those allegorical, political songs, so common in Ireland. The poet
sings of his country under the similitude of a distressed maiden, to
whom he is ardently attached. In the allusions to the Pope and
clergy, we behold the hopes of obtaining assistance from the Catholic

Like drifted snow the mountain's breast that presses—
    The cuckoo's notes resound,
    In winter, where thou 'rt found,
Beloved of the flaxen tresses!

III.

    Oh! if the boon were mine,
    From beauty's ranks divine,
To choose for aye the fairest maiden,
    'Twere her to whom sweet lays
    Consign the palm of praise,
For whom a thousand hearts with love are laden.
    Such maid did once inspire
    The Hebrew monarch's lyre;
But, oh! thine eye more dignity expresses—
    Relieve my woe, I crave;
    Oh! snatch me from the grave,
Beloved of the flaxen tresses!

——:o:——

ROS GEAL DUBH.

I.

A long, long way since yesterday
    I wildly sped,
O'er mountain steep and valley deep,
    With airy tread;

powers of Europe. The concluding stanza vividly shews the bloody struggle that would take place ere Rose, his beloved Ireland, would be yielded to the foe. Hardiman's "Minstrelsy" has a different form of this song, but this is the popular version in the south, and is said to be as old as the time of Elizabeth.

Loċ Eipne ʒo léimfṅn,
    Cé ʒup móp í ap ṁṅp,
ʒap am ṫiaiṫ máp ʒile ʒṅéine
    Aċṫ mo Róp ʒeal ᴅuḃ!

II.

ʒo ᴅ-ṫí'n áonaċ má ṫéiʒean ṫú
    A ᴅíol ᴅo pṫuic,
Ṁa ṫéiʒean ṫú, ná fap ᴅéaʒnaċ
    'S ap oíᴅċe amṅʒ;
Bioṫ bolṫaiṫ aip ᴅo ḃoippe,
    Ip móp ʒlap-cip,
Nó ap baoʒal ᴅṅṫ ap Cléipeaċ
    ᴅo'n Róp ʒeal ᴅuḃ!

III.

A Róipín na bioṫ bpóp opṫ,
    Na cáp apoip,
Ṫá ᴅo ṗápᴅún óp Róiṁ
    Ip óp ṗápa aʒum,
Ṫá na bpáiṫpe ṫeaċṫ ṫap páile,
    Ip a ᴅ-ṫpiall ṫap mṅp,
Ip ní ceilfeap fíop Spáipeaċ aip
    Ṁo Róp ʒeal ᴅuḃ!

IV.

Ṫa ʒpáṫ aʒam am láp ᴅṅṫ
    Le bliaʒaip apoip,
ʒpáṫ cpáiṫe, ʒpáṫ capṁap,
    ʒpáṫ ciopaṫa,

Loch Earne's tide, though its wave be wide,
    I'd leap above,
Were my guiding light that sunburst bright,
    The *Rós geal dubh !*

II.

If to the fair you would repair
    To sell your flocks,
I pray secure your every door
    With bolts and locks ;
Nor linger late from the guarded gate,
    When abroad you rove,
Or the clerk will play through the live-long day,
    With *Rós geal dubh !*

III.

My dearest Rose, why should these woes
    Dishearten thee ?
The Pope of Rome hath sent thee home
    A pardon free—
A priestly train, o'er the briny main,
    Shall greet my love,
And wine of Spain to thy health we'll drain,
    My *Rós geal dubh !*

IV.

My love sincere is centred here
    This year and more—
Love sadly vexing, love perplexing,
    Love painful, sore,

Ᵹᵽáꝺ ꝺ'ꝼáᵹ ṁé ᵹaη ꞃláιηꞇe,
    Ᵹaη ṗιaη, ᵹaη ᵽꞃᵹꞇ,
Jꞃ ᵹo bꞃaꞇ, bꞃaꞇ ᵹaη aoη ꝼaιll aᵹaṁ
    Aιꞃ Ꞃóꞃ ᵹeal ꝺuḃ !

v.

Ꝺo ꞃιúḃaꝼlaιηηꞃι aη Ɯuṁaη leaꞇ,
    Jꞃ cιúṁιaꞃ ηa ᵹ-cηoc,
Ɯaη ꞃṁl ᵹo ḃ-ꝼaιᵹιηη ꞃúη oꞃꞇ
    No páιꞃꞇ le cιoη ;
A cꞃáoḃ cꞃꞄꞇa, ꞇuᵹꞇaꞃ ꝺṁηηe,
    Ᵹo ḃ-ꝼṁl ᵹꞃáꝺ aᵹuꞇ ꝺaṁ ;
Jꞃ ᵹuη b'ι plúꞃ-ꞃᵹoιꞇ ηa ṁ-baη ṁṁηꞇe,
    Ɯo Ꞃóꞃ ᵹeal ꝺuḃ !

vi.

Béιꝺ aη ꝼaꞃaιᵹe ηa ꞇꞃιlꞇe ꝺeaꞃᵹa,
    Jꞃ aη ꞃpéιꞃ ηa ꝼṁl,
Béιꝺ aη ꞃaoᵹal ηa coᵹa cꞃaoꞃaċ,
    Ꝺo ꝺꞃᵹṁ ηa ᵹ-cηoc,
Béιꝺ ᵹaċ ᵹleaηη ꞃléιḃe aιꞃ ꝼuꝺ Eιꞃeaηη,
    A'ꞃ móιηꞇe aιꞃ cꞃιꞇ,
Lá éιᵹιη ꞃul a η-éaᵹꝼaιꝺ
    Ɯo Ꞃóꞃ ᵹeal ꝺuḃ !

Love, whose rigour hath crush'd my vigour,
 Thrice hopeless love,
While fate doth sever me ever, ever,
 From *Rós geal dubh !*

v.

Within thy heart could I claim a part,
 One secret share—
We'd shape our flight, o'er the wild hills' height,
 Towards Munster fair ;
Branch of beauty's tree, it seems to me
 I have thy love—
And the mildest flower of hall or bower,
 Is *Rós geal dubh !*

vi.

The sea outspread shall be raging red,
 All blood the skies—
And crimson war shall shout afar
 Where the wild hills rise—
Each mountain glen and mossy fen,
 In fear shall move,
Some future day, ere thou pass away,
 My *Rós geal dubh !*

BAN-CHNOIC EIREAN OĠ.*

I.

Is fairsing 's fáilteaċ an áit do ḃeiṫ a n-Eirinn,
Uileacán duḃ O!
Mar a m-bíḋeann toraḋ na sláinte a m bárr na déise ann,
Uileacán duḃ O!
Bíḋeann an ṁil air an g-crann aṅ, a n-gleaṅtaiḃ ceoiḋ,
'S na sruṫa is an t-saṁra ann, a g-ciuṁais gaċ róid,
Bíḋeaṅ uisge 'n a ṡruill ann, a's drúċd am nóin,
Air ḃán-ċnoic Eirean oġ!

II.

Is baċallaċ, buacaċ, dualaċ dréimneaċ,
Uileacán duḃ O!
Gaċ fanaire a ġlúaiseas ó ċúantaiḃ na h-Eirean,
Ulieacán duḃ O!
Raċfadsa air cuaird, má's buan mo ṡaoġal ḃéiḋeas,
Go talaṁ an trúairceas mar ar dual do ṡaoġal ḃeiṫ,
Do b'fearr liom 'ná ḃur n-dualgas gíḋ mór le mṅiḋeaṁ ḃeiṫ,
Air ḃán-ċnoic Eirean óg!

* *Ban-chnoic Eirean ógh*, literally *the fair Hills of Virgin Ireland.* This song speaks the ardent love of the Irish exile for

THE FAIR HILLS OF EIRE OGH.

I.

Beautiful and wide are the green fields of Erin,
      Uileacán dubh O!
With life-giving grain in the golden corn therein,
      Uileacán dubh O!
And honey in the woods of the mist-wreaths deep,
And in the summer by the paths the bright streams
    leap,
At burning noon, rich, sparkling dew the fair flowers
    steep,
      On the fair hills of Eire Ogh!

II.

How clustering his ringlets, how lofty his bearing,
      Uileacán dubh O!
Each warrior leaving the broad bays of Erin,
      Uileacán dubh O!
Would heaven grant the hope in my bosom swelling,
I'd seek that land of joy in life's gifts excelling,
Beyond your rich rewards, I'd choose a lowly dwel-
    ling,
      On the fair hills of Eire Ogh!

his native land.   It is said to have been written by an Irish student
in one of the colleges of France.

III.

Jɼ ᴅαɼɓeαc 'ɼ jɼ ṁóɼ jαᴅ cɼυαċα ɲα ɧ-ℰjɼeαñ,
     Ujleαcáɲ ᴅυɓ O!
Bjᴅeαɲɲ αɲ ᴅ-jṁ α'ɼ αɲ ᴅíιαċᴅαɼ αʒ ʒlυαjɼeαċᴅ
    'ɲα ɼlαoᴅ αɲɲ,
     Ujleαcáɲ ᴅυɓ O!
Bjᴅeαñ αɲ bjollαɼ αjɼ αɲ ᴅ-ᴅojɲɲ αɲɲ α'ɼ ɼαñjαᴅ
   boʒ ɼóʒαjl,
21'ɼ ɲα cυαċα αʒ lαbαjɼᴅ αɲɲ ó ló ʒo ló,
'S αɲ ɼṁójljɲ υαɼαl jɼ ꜰυαjṁ-bjɲɲe ceól,
    21jɼ báɲ-ċɲojc ℰjɼeαñ óʒ!

———:o:———

uαjll cυṁαjꝺ 2ιɴ ϻ2ιɴʒ2ιɼℰ sυʒ2ιċ.[*]

I.

21 ᴅαlᴅα ᴅjl αɲ ᴅαjɲjᴅ leαᴅ mo ċáɼ αɲojɼ,
21ṁ ċαɼᴅα αʒ αɲ ℰαʒlαjɼ ʒαɲ ꝼáɼᴅ αjɼ bjċ,
21ɲ αjcṁe ɼeo ɲj ʒlαcαjᴅ me αċᴅ αṁ ꝼáʒαɲαjɼe,
'S ɲj ʒαbαjᴅ ljoṁ αṁ Phɼoᴅeɼᴅαɲᴅ 'ɲα'ṁ Pháραjɼe!

II.

Φejɼ ꝼeαɼɼα'cα ʒυɼ ceαɼαṁαċ ɲeαṁ-ʒɲájᴅɼeαċ
   ṁé,
'S cé ʒo ɲ-αᴅbαjṁ ʒυɼ Saʒɼαɲαċ ᴅα láᴅαjɼ ṁé,

---

[*] Andrew Magrath, commonly called the *Mangaire Sugach*, or
Jolly Merchant, having been expelled from the Roman Catholic
Church for his licentious life, offered himself as a convert to the

III.

Gainful and large are the corn-stacks of Erin,
  Uileacán dubh O!
Yellow cream and butter abound ever therein
  Uileacán dubh O!
And sorrel soft and cresses where bright streams stray,
And speaking cuckoos fill the grove the live-long day,
And the little thrush so noble of sweetest-sounding
 lay,
  On the fair hills of Eire ogh!

——:o:——

LAMENT OF THE MANGAIRE SUGACH.

I.

Beloved! do you pity not my doleful case—
Pursu'd by priest and minister in dire disgrace;
The Churchmen brand the vagabond upon my brow,
O! they'll take me not as Protestant or Papist now!

II.

The parson calls me wanderer and homeless knave—
And though I boast the Saxon creed with aspect
 grave,

doctrines of Protestantism; but the Protestant clergyman having
also refused to accept him, the unfortunate *Mangaire* gave vent to
his feelings in this lament.

Ⅾeiɲ 'ɲ úaiɲ ɾᵹaɲaɱ leiɾ ᵹuɲ aᵹ Aiꝼⲛⲓoɲɲ iꞃ ᵹɲáiṫ
    íṫe ɱé,
'S ɲaċ ceaċ꤫aɲ ꞃⲓⲛ ɱe, Pꞃoⲧeꞃⲧaⲛⲧ ɲa Pápaiɲe !

III.

Ⅾeaɲbaɲ ᵹaɲ ṫéaꞃɱa꤫ ɲaċ ꝼuláiꞃ leiꞃ ɱé,
Ⅾo ċaꞃⲧa ɲoiꞃ le h-aċⲧaɲa ꤫o láṫaiꞃ, ceiɲⲧ
Ɜo ꞃaċa lⲓoɱ ċuɱ aċaɲaiɲɲ ᵹaɲ ꞃꝑáꞃ aiꞃ bⲓⲧ,
'S ᵹo ᵹ-caiṫꝼea꤫ beiṫ aɱ Phꞃoⲧeꞃⲧaⲛⲧ ɲo aⲛ
    Phápaiɲe !

IV.

Aⲛ Saᵹaꞃⲧ ꤫eiꞃ ᵹuꞃ ꝼeaɲɲaiꞃe ɲeaṁ-áṫbaꞃac ɱé,
'S ᵹo ꤫-ⲧaꞃaiɲᵹíɱ le ɱaɲᵹaiꞃeaċ꤫ ɲa ɱɲá ċuⲛ
    ꞃⲓⲗⲥ ;
Ɜuꞃ ɱeaꞃa ɱé ɲa ꝼóᵹaiꞃe aⲧa le bꞃoⲓꝺ,
'S ɲaċ ᵹabaⲓꝺ lⲓoɱ aɱ Phꞃoⲧeꞃⲧaⲛⲧ ɲa 'ɱ Phá-
    paiɲe !

V.

A ꤫eiꞃ ꤫á ꝼꞃeaᵹꞃa꤫ ᵹuꞃ eaċ꤫aɲaċ ᵹaɲ ɲáiꞃe ɱé,
'S ɲaċ ⲧaiṫɱⲓoɱaċ ɱo beaꞃⲧa ɲá ɱo ċáiⲗe leiꞃ ;
Naċ aiṫꞃeaċ ɱe aċꝺ ꞃacaiꞃe aⲧa ᵹaɲ ꞃⲧꞃuꞃ,
A ċleaċꝺaꞃ beiṫ aɱ Pꞃoⲧeꞃⲧaⲛⲧ 'ꞃ aⲛ Phápaiɲe !

VI.

Ní ċaꞃⲧaɲaċꝺ ꝼá ꤫eaꞃa ꤫ó ɲá ᵹꞃáiɲ ꤫o ꞃ̇ulⲧ,
Aⲙⲟ beaꞃⲧaꞃa ꤫o ṫaᵹꞃa ꤫o láṫaiɱ Sᵹoⲓⲧ,
Ní ɱeaꞃꝺa ꤫ó ɱo ṁaꞃlaꞃa a ᵹ-cáꞃ aiꞃ bⲓⲧ,
Be aca ꞃⲓⲛ ɱe Pꞃoⲧeꞃⲧaⲛⲧ ɲó Pápaiɲe !

He says that claim my Popish face must disallow,
Although I'm neither Protestant nor Papist now!

III.

He swears (and oh! he'll keep his oath) he's firmly
· bent
To hunt me down by penal Acts of Parliament;
Before the law's coercive might to make me bow,
And choose between the Protestant and Papist
now!

IV.

The priest me deems a satirist of luckless lay,
Whose merchant-craft hath often led fair maids
astray;
And worse than hunted fugitive all disavow,
He'll take me not a Protestant or Papist now!

V.

That further, I'm a foreigner devoid of shame,
Of hateful, vile, licentious life, and evil name;
A ranting, rhyming wanderer, without a cow,
Who now is deem'd a Protestant—a Papist now!

VI.

Alas! it was not charity or Christian grace
That urged to drag my deeds before the Scotic race—
What boots it him to write reproach upon my brow,
Whether they deem me Protestant or Papist now?

VII.

Cᴀ ꝼᴀᴅᴀ ᴅo bᴊ Ꝡᴀӡᴅᴀleɲ ɪꞃ Ɖᴀᴊbᴊ ᴀɲ Ƀᴊӡ,
Ꝉɪɲ ꞅeᴀꞃᴀbᴀll, ɪꞃ Pól ᴀbꞃᴛᴀl ċꞃɲ ɲᴀ ᴛᴀɪɲᴛe ᴀ
   ꝙ-bꞃoɪᴅ,
Ɖo ӡlᴀcᴀᴛ́ ɪᴀᴅ ɲuᴀɪꞃ ċᴀꞃᴀᴅᴀꞃ ᴀ ӡ-cᴀᴊl ꝼᴀ ӡ-cɪoɲ,
Ɉꞃ ceᴀċᴅᴀꞃ ᴅᴊob ɲᴊoꞃ Pꞃoᴛeꞃᴛᴀɲᴛ ɲᴀ Pᴀpᴀɪɲe!

VIII.

Oꞃ ꝼeᴀꞃᴀċ ꝑé ᴀɪꞃ ᴅeᴀꞃꝳᴀᴅ ӡᴀɲ ꝼᴀɪᴛ ӡᴀɲ ꝼɪoꞃ,
Ɉꞃ ӡuꞃ ꝼᴀᴅᴀ ꝑe ᴀɪꞃ ꝯeᴀꞃᴀbᴀll ӡᴀɲ ᴀɪᴛ ᴀɪꞃ bɪᴛ,
Cᴀɪᴛꝼɪoᴅ cuꞃ le h-ᴀᴛᴀꞃᴀċ ɲᴀ ᴅ-ᴛᴀɪɲᴛe ꞃɪɲ,
Ɖo ӡᴀbᴀꞃ lɪoꝳ ᴀꝳ Pꞃꞃoᴛeꞃᴛᴀɲᴛ ɲo'ꝳ Pꞅᴀpᴀɪɲe!

IX.

Ꝉ ᴅᴀlᴛᴀ ᴅɪl, cᴀ ꞃᴀċᴀᴅꞃᴀ ċuꝳ ꝼᴀӡᴀɪɲ ᴀɲoɪꞃ,
O cᴀᴛᴀᴛ́ ꝑé ᴀꞃ ᴀɲ ɛᴀӡlᴀɪꞃ 'ꞃӡo ᴅ-ᴛᴀꞃlᴀ 'ꝳꞃӡ;
Cᴀɪᴛꝼeᴀᴅ beɪᴛ ᴀꝳ Cᴀlbɪꞃɪꞃᴛ ɲo'ꝳ Ꝉɪꞃɪᴀɲ oɪlc,
O ꞃӡᴀꞃᴀꞃ beɪᴛ ᴀꝳ Pꞃꞃoᴛeꞃᴛᴀɲᴛ ɲo'ꝳ Pꞅᴀpᴀɪɲe!

Ꝉɲ Ceᴀɲӡᴀl.

Ꝼéᴀċ ᴀɲ ᴛ'ᴀbꞃᴛᴀl Peᴀᴅᴀɪꞃ ᴅo ꝑeᴀcᴀɪᴛ́ ꝼᴀ ᴛꞃᴊ ᴀɪꞃ
   ᴅ-ᴛꞃᴊꞃ,
Ꝉӡ ꞃéᴀꞃᴀᴛ́ ᴀ ċᴀꞃᴀɪᴅ ӡuꞃ ӡlᴀcᴀᴛ́ ᴀꞃᴊꞃ ӡo h-úꝳᴀl;
'Sᴀ Ɖᴊᴀ ᴅɪl ᴀċɲꞃꝳ ce ꞃӡᴀꞃᴀꞃ le ᴛlᴊӡe ɲᴀ ɲ-úꞃᴅ,
Ꝡᴀꞃ ᴀoɲ le Peᴀᴅᴀɪꞃ ᴀɲ Ꝡᴀɲӡᴀɪꞃe ꞃӡᴀoɪl ᴀᴅ ᴅúɲ!

VII.

Lo ! David, Israel's poet-king and Magdaléne,
And Paul, who of the Christian creed the foe had
    been—
Did Heaven, when sorrow fill'd their heart, reject their
    vow,
Though they were neither Protestant nor Papist now ?

VIII.

O ! since I weep my wretched heart to evil prone,
A wanderer in the paths of sin, all lost and lone—
At other shrines with other flocks I fain must bow,
Who'll take me, whether Protestant or Papist now !

IX.

Beloved ! whither can I flee for peace at last,
When thus beyond the Church's pale I'm rudely cast?
The Arian creed or Calvinist I must avow,
When sever'd from the Protestant and Papist now !

THE SUMMING-UP.

See Peter th' Apostle, whose lapses from grace were
    three,
Denying the Saviour, was granted a pardon free—
O God! though the *Mangairé* from him thy mild laws
    cast,
Receive him, like Peter, to dwell in THY HOUSE at
    last !

CUPAN UJ Ḃ-eaзRa.*

Ceaṗballán ṗó ċáṅ.

I.

Ɖa ṁ-béṙöiṅṅṙj aṁṅċ a ṅ-ᴁṗajṅ
Nó a ṅ-заṗ Ꝝleaṅṅ-ṅa-ḟéuᴅ
ᴁ)aṗ a ṅ-зlúajṙeaṅṅ заċ ṙáṗ-loṅз
˙˙ le cláṗéaᴅ a'ṙ le ṁéaᴅ
B'ḟeáṗṗ ljoṁ é ṁaṗ ṙáṙaṁ
ᴁзuṙ ḟáзajṁ é ᴅaṁ ḟéjṅ
Cupáṅ зeal Uj eaзṗa
ᴁзuṙ ḟáзajl láṅ le ṁo ɓeul!

II.

Caᴅ é b'ájll ljoṁ 'з á ċuṗ a з-céjl
'S a ljaċᴛ ájз ṁajᴛ 'ṅ a ᴅejз,
Jṙ зuṗ b'é ᴅejṗ ollᴅáṁ ṅa ḃ-ájᴛe
Ɖaṗ ṁo láṁṙa ṅj bṅéuз—
Ċojṗᴅealɓajċ Ḃṗjajṅ aзaṁajl
Ꞇaṗ ᴛṗáċ ḟa ṁo ᴅéjṅ
Ꝝo ṅ-ólḟaṁ aṙ aṅ ᴛ-ṙáṗ-ċupáṅ
Slájṅᴛe ɓṗeáз Ċéjṅ.

* *Cupán ui Eaghra, the Cup of O'Hara.* This is one of the celebrated Carolan's songs, and was composed by the harper to celebrate the hospitality of Kean O'Hara, a gentleman of ancient family in the County Sligo.

THE CUP OF O'HARA.

I.

Were I over in Arran,
  Or wild Glan-na-Séud,
Where tall barks of swiftness
  Bear claret and mead ;
'Twere joy to my bosom,
  In gladness to sip
O'Hara's bright wine-cup,
  Fill'd high to my lip !

II.

Why praise what is sought for
  By old man and youth,
While the doctors and sages
  (By this hand I am sooth)
Cry, Turlogh, sweet harper,
  Come timely to drain
That costly, tall wine-cup,
  To the health of brave Kean !

ᴀ Rᴀıḃ ᴄu ᴀꝝ ᴀn ꝝ-CᴀRRᴀıꝝ ? *

I.

ᴀn ꝛᴀıḃ ᴄú ᴀꝝ ᴀn ꝝ-Cᴀꝛꝛᴀıꝝ, nó ḃ-ꝼᴀcᴀ ᴄú ꝼéıṁ mo
ꝝꝛáḋ,

Nó ᴀ ḃ-ꝼᴀcᴀ ᴄú ꝝıle, ꝼınne, ᴀꝝuꝛ ꝛꝝéıṁ nᴀ mná,

Nó ᴀ ḃ-ꝼᴀcᴀ ᴄú ᴀn ᴄ-uḃᴀl ḃᴀ cúḃᴀꝛᴄᴀ ıꝛ ḃᴀ ṁıllꝛe
ḃláᴄ,

Nó ᴀ ḃ-ꝼᴀcᴀ ᴄú mo ḃᴀlᴀnᴄıne nó ᴀ ḃ-ꝼꝛıl ꝛı ᴅ'ᴀ
clᴀoıᴅ mᴀꝛ ᴄáım ?

II.

Ꝺo ḃıoꝛᴀ ᴀꝝ ᴀn ꝝ-Cᴀꝛꝛᴀıꝝ, ıꝛ ᴅo ċonᴀıꝛc me ꝼéın
ᴅo ꝝꝛáḋ,

Ꝺo ċonᴀıꝛc mé ꝝıle, ꝼınne, ᴀꝝuꝛ ꝛꝝéıṁ nᴀ mná,

Ꝺo ċonᴀıꝛc mé ᴀn ᴄuḃᴀl ḃᴀ cúḃᴀꝛᴄᴀ ıꝛ ḃᴀ ṁıllꝛe
ḃláᴄ,

Ꝺo ċonᴀıꝛc mé ᴅo ḃᴀlᴀnᴄın ᴀꝝuꝛ nı'l ꝛı ᴅᴀ clꝛoıᴅ
mᴀꝛ ᴄáıꝛ !

III.

Iꝛ ꝼıú cꝛꝝ ꝝꝛneᴀ ꝝᴀċ ꝛıḃe ᴅᴀ ꝝꝛuᴀıꝝ mᴀꝛ óꝛ,

Iꝛ ꝼıú oıꝛeᴀᴅ eıle ᴀ cꝛᴅeᴀċᴄᴀ úᴀıꝛ ꝛᴀıḃ ló ;

ᴀ cúılın ᴄꝛom ᴄꝛıꝛꝛılıċ ᴀ ᴄꝛꝝᴄıꝛ léı ꝛıoꝛ ꝝo ꝼeóıꝛ

'Sᴀ ċuᴀıċın nᴀ ꝼınne, ᴀn ṁıꝛᴄe ᴅo ꝛláꝛnᴄe ᴅ'ól?

---

* This is a song of the South, but there are so many places of the
name of Carrick, such as Carrick-on-Shannon, Carrick-on-Suir, &c.,
that I cannot fix its precise locality. In this truly Irish song, when
the pining swain learns that his absent mistress is not love-sick
like himself, he praises the beauty of her copious hair, throws off a

HAVE YOU BEEN AT CARRICK?

I.

Have you been at Carrick, and saw you my true-love
there?

And saw you her features, all beautiful, bright, and
fair?

Saw you the most fragrant, flowering, sweet apple-
tree?—

O! saw you my lov'd one, and pines she in grief like
me?

II.

I have been at Carrick, and saw thy own true-love
there;

And saw, too, her features, all beautiful, bright, and
fair;

And saw the most fragrant, flowering, sweet apple-
tree—

I saw thy lov'd one—she pines not in grief, like thee!

III.

Five guineas would price every tress of her golden
hair—

Then think what a treasure her pillow at night to
share,

These tresses thick-clustering and curling around
her brow—

O, Ringlet of Fairness! I'll drink to thy beauty now!

glass to her health, enumerates his sufferings, and swears to forego
the sex for ever; but she suddenly bursts upon his view, his resolves
vanish into thin air, and he greets his glorious maid with such a
welcome as an Irish lover alone can give!

IV.

'N úair ḃím-se am ċoḋla bían osnaḋ gan bríġ am
ċliaḃ,
Is mé am luiḋ eadar cnocaiḃ go d-tigiḋ an dúaċ
aniar;
A rúin ḋil s'a ċogair ní'l fortaċt mo ċúis aċt Dia,
Is go n-deanaḋ loċ fola do ḟolus mo ṡúl ad ḋiaiḋ!

V.

Is go d-tigiḋ an ċáisg air lár an ḟoġṁair buiḋe,
Is lá ḟéil Pátruig lá nó ḋó na ḋiaiġ,
Go b-fása an bláṫ bán tre lár mo ċoṁra ċaol,
Páirt da gráḋ go braṫ ní ṫabarfad do ṁnaoi!

VI.

Siúd í síos an Ríoġ-bean áluinn óg,
A bfuil a gruaig léi sgaoilte síos go béal a bróg,
S í an eala í mar an litir do ṡiolraiġ ón t-sár fuil
ṁór,
Ċaraid ġeal mo ċroiḋe, céad míle fáilte roṁat!

IV.

When seeking to slumber, my bosom is rent with
    sighs—
I toss on my pillow till morning's blest beams arise ;
No aid, bright Beloved! can reach me save GOD above,
For a blood-lake is form'd of the light of my eyes with
    love !

V.

Until yellow Autumn shall usher the Paschal day,
And Patrick's gay festival come in its train alway—
Until through my coffin the blossoming boughs shall
    grow,
My love on another I'll never in life bestow !

VI.

Lo! yonder the maiden illustrious, queen-like, high,
With long-flowing tresses adown to her sandal-tie—
Swan, fair as the lily, descended of high degree,
A myriad of welcomes, dear maid of my heart, to thee !

NORA AN ĊUJL OṀRA.

I.

A Nóра an ċúl ómра,
'Sé mo bráónра naċ b-реrσаim
Láṁ σo ċrр раоj 'σ ċeann-ра,
Nó a m-bpollaċ σo léjne;
Jr тú σ-ḟáз mo ċeann-ра
Зan ŕηра ajp bjт céjlle,
A'r зo η-éalóċajnn тan тоjnn leaт,
A pḟη-ṙeapc σá b-реrσрajnn!

II.

A bajll jηтjnn ċрojσe rтjз,
Ná σéanра ljoṁ bpéaз,
A'r зup зeall тú mo pórаσ
Зan реоjрljnn 'r an π-rаoзal;
Sjúbajlṙjnnre ajp an η-bпúċσ leaт,
A'r nj bрήзṙjnn leaт an реrp;
A'r a Nóра an ċúl ómра,
Jr σear a pózраjnn σo berl!

III.

Тaоḃ тall σe'n Aṁuajσ
Тá rтóр зeal mo ċрojσe
A cŕl тjuз map an т-ómap
Lé 'p ċajll mé mo зnaojσ
Зạσjm-rj Rjз an σoṁnajċ
Зo σ-тjonnтojзe an зaoт,
A'r зo b-реjcjσ mé mo bólaċт
Aз зaḃajl bójтpe Bajle-áт bрзσe.

AMBER-HAIR'D NORA.

I.

O ! amber-hair'd Nora,
   That thy fair head could rest
On the arm that would shelter
   Or circle thy breast !
Thou hast stolen all my brain, love,
   And then left me lone—
Though I'd cross o'er the main, love,
   To call thee mine own !

II.

Why, maid of my bosom,
   Should falsehood be thine ?
Thou hast promis'd to wed me,
   Though wealth were not mine ;
The dew-sprinkled grass, love,
   Scarce feels my light feet,
And, amber-hair'd Nora,
   My kisses are sweet !

III.

My fair one is dwelling
   By Moy's lovely vale—
Her rich locks of amber
   Have left my cheek pale—
May the king of the Sabbath
   Yet grant me to see
My herds in the green lanes
   Of fair Baile-ath-Buidhe !

AN BḢRUINNEALL MḢEIRBḢ.

I.

Maioin ceóoaċ nuaiṛ o'éiṛiʒeaṛ,
Iṛ ċuaoaṛ amaċ ṗá'n ʒ-coill ʒlaṛ,
Iṛ ann oo búail an cṛéiʒio mé
    Naċ leiʒiṛṗeaṛ, ṗaṛaon ;
Do ċuala an bṛuiñeall ṁeióṛeaċ,
A líʒb na coille oṛoiʒneaċ,
Do ṗṛeab mo ċṛoioe le ʒṛeañ oi,
    Ʒuṛ oéiʒ-bean oaṁ í !

II.

'N uaiṛ ʒabaiṁre amaċ na bánoa,
Aʒuṛ ċióiṁre uaiṁ mo ʒṛáo ʒeal,
A oṛeaċ maṛ ṛóṛ a n-ʒáiṛoín,
    Iṛ bláċ ʒeal na n-ṛ́ball,
Iṛ bṛeaʒa í na Venus
An can o'ṗáʒ ṛí an cṛeun-ṁṛṛ ;
A oá cíċ ċṛuiñe caoṁa,
    'S aṛ éaonom a ṛiúbal !

III.

'Sé oo ʒṛáoṛa ċlaoióiʒ mé,
'S iṛ maiṛʒ áic a m-bioean ṛé !
Cṛṛean ṛe a nṛ́ṁail oon c-ʒaoʒal ṛo,
    An ċnoio oo ʒṇio an ʒṛáo,
Iṛ ṗaoa oaṁ oá ṗoiʒneaṁ,
Aċ caiṛṗeao ṗeaṛoa é íṛṛn,
Ʒuṛ 'bé oo ʒṛáoṛa ṁeall mé,
    Naċ b-ṗaiʒio mé ʒo bṛáċ !

THE GRACEFUL MAIDEN.

I.

One morn when mists did hover
The green-wood's foliage over,
'Twas then I did discover
      How painful love may be ;
A maid, 'mid shades concealing,
Pour'd forth her voice of feeling,
And love came o'er me stealing,
      She's a dear maid to me !

II.

When through the valleys roaming,
I see my bright love coming,
Like garden-rose all blooming,
      Or flower of the apple-tree ;
Bright Venus she's excelling
Fresh from her ocean-dwelling,
Her soft, round bosom swelling,
      Her foot-falls light and free.

III.

" Thy love hath left me dying ;
The heart where love is lying
Will find what torment trying
      Round ruin'd hopes may twine ;
And long I've borne the token,
But now it must be spoken,
How thou my heart hast broken,
      Who never canst be mine !"

IV.

Ꙋ óɪჳ-ꝼɪn áɪჳ, ꝺa m-ꝼéɪꝺɪn
Ʒo m' ꝼɪnɪnne ꝺo ɾჳéalɾa,
Ꝺo leɪჳɪɾꝼɪn ꝼéɪn ó'n b-ꝼéɪn ꞇú,
Ꝺa m-béɪꝺɪn lɪom a ꝛúɲ;
Ꞇá mo ċaꝛaɪꝺ aɪɾ ჳaċ ꞇaob ꝺɪom,
Ꙋ'ɾ coꝛuჳaꝺ amaċ nɪ ꝼéaꝺaɪm,
Ꙋċ cꝛꝛɪꝺ cunꝺaɾ ჳeuɾ oꝛ'm
Ca ꝺ-ꞇéɪჳɪmɾe ċum ɾɪ́ꝛbaɪl.

V.

Ꙋɪꞇꝛɪɾ ꝺóɪb, a ɾꝼéɪn beaɲ,
Ʒo ꝛaċꝼaɪɾ ɾeal aჳ aeꝛɪჳeaċꞇ,
Ʒo b-ꝼꝛɪl ꞇú ꞇꝛꝛɾeaċ ꞇꝛéɪꞇ-laჳ,
Ꙋ'ɾ ꝺ'ɪꞚꞇɪꞚ ჳo ꝺubaċ;
Ʒeabaɪꝺ ꞇꝛ́ mɪɾe, am aonaɾ,
Ꙋ lꞚb na coɪlle cꝛaobꝛჳe;
Ꙋ'ɾ ჳo ꝺeɪꞚɪn ma ꝺéanaɪɾ bꝛéaჳ lɪom,
Ꙋ'ɾ ꞇaoɾ oɾꞇ mo ċꝛ̇ɾ!

VI.

Ꙋ'ɾ ɪomꝺa ჳeallamꞚ́n bꝛéɪჳe,
Ꝺo ċuჳ ꞇú ɲɪam ó'ꝺ béal ꝺam,
Ꝼaꝺ beɪꞇ ჳɾɪaɲ aɪɾ aeꝺaɾ,
Ꙋჳuɾ ꝼeuɾ ჳlaɾ a ꝼáɾ;
Ʒo ꝺ-ꞇꝛeabꝼaċ caoɪɾe maola,
Ꙋɪɾ ċꝛ́l a ჳ-cɪɲɲ, na ɾléɪbꞇe,
Naċ ɲ-ꝺéanꝼaꝺ m' aꞇꝛuჳaꝺ ċéɪle,
Ꙋ'ɾ ꝼéaċ anoɪɾ maɾ ꞇá!

IV.

" O ! thou of misery telling,
  If truth thy tongue's impelling,
  I'd ease the pain that's quelling
        Thy life, were mine the cure.
  But watchful friends surround me,
  With promise strict they've bound me,
  And if they wandering found me,
        What ills might I endure !"

v.

" Tell them, O, light-limb'd maiden,
  Thy bloom with grief is fading—
  Where groves are foliage-laden,
        Thou'lt stray all lonelily :
  I'll for thy coming pine, love,
  Where the dark wood's boughs entwine, love,
  And O ! what guilt is thine, love,
        If false thou be to me !"

VI.

" Alas ! how oft thou'st riven
  The vow thy lips had given,
  While shone the light of heaven,
        Or verdure deck'd the plain,
  Till sheep, each silly rover,
  Would plough the mountains over,
  Thou wouldst be my true lover—
        But lo ! the hope is vain !"

VII.

Ʒléaꞃꝼaıꝺ mé lonʒ ꞃeólꞇaıꝺe,
Ꝺ'ꞃ ꞃaċꝼaıꝺ mé ʒo Ꝼlanꝺꞃꞅꞅ,
Ꝺ meaꞃʒ na ꞇ-ꞇıoꞃꞇa ʒallꝺa,
Ꝺ'ꞃ na ꝺıaıꝺ ꞃn ꞃaıʒeaꝺ ꝺon Sꞃáın—
Ꝺ ṁaıʒꝺean ṁaıꞃıʒ, ṁoꝺṁaꞃaıʒ,
Nı ꝼıllꝼıꝺ mé nıoꞃ mó oꞃꞇ,
Bıoꝺ ꝺo ꞃoʒa ꝼeaꞃ ꞃóꞃꝺa aʒaꝺ,
Ꝺo ꞃóṁaꞃꝼaıꝺ ꝺꞃꞇ an bán!

———:o:———

ꝺuꝺN ꝺN Ḃꝺꝺoꞃꝺ.*

I.

Ꝺ ḃaꞃc b'aꞃaṁ ꞇꞃ a n-aꞃacaıꞃ na ꞇ-ꞇoꞃꞃaꞃaċ
ꞃ-áꞃꝺ,
Cáıꞃʒ coḃaꞃꞇaċ ʒıꝺ buꝺ baꞃḃaꞃꝺa ꞇꞃoṁ é aꞃ lá,
Ꞇꞃáꞇ laꞃaıꝺ an ꝼaıꞃʒe ó ḃonn ʒo báꞃ,
Lán coꞃꞃ ꝺı nı ʒaḃaꞃ ó ꞃꞇꞃꞃ ʒo cꞃaꞃꞃ!

Cꞃꞃ ꝼa.

Ꝺ báꞃ a lán, a báꞃ a lán,
Ꝺ ʒꞃáꝺ na ꞃꞃn, a ċꞃꝺ ꝺe'ꞃ ꞇ-ꞃaoʒal,
Ꝺ lán—'ꞃı an báꝺ bꞃeaꝺ ꞃeoıl!

---

* *Duan an Bhadóra, the Boatman's Song.* I have copied this spirited sea-song from the second volume of Mr. Hardiman's "Minstrelsy," where it is left untranslated. Mr. Hardiman says

VII.

"And now, with white sails flowing,
  To Flanders I'll be going;
I'll seek the vineyards growing
    In distant Gaul and Spain—
Proud maid, no more I'll woo thee,
No more with love pursue thee;
Another mate may sue thee,
    And plough for thee the plain !"

——:o:——

THE BOAT SONG.

I.

Bark, scorning every peril of the angry spray,
Safe shelter mid the terrors of the storm com-
  pass'd way ;
When yawning billows redly roll from ocean's cave,
From stern unto quivering mast she ships no wave !

CHORUS.

A flowing tide, a flowing tide,
My secret love, my worldly store,
Flowing—my brave sailing boat !

that this marine ode is " well known along many parts of the Irish
coast, but particularly the west." A translation of this and other
Irish songs, by Mr. (now Sir) Samuel Ferguson, will be found in
the *Dublin University Magazine* for November, 1834.

II.

Τρáċ ġléaɼɼaɲɲ ɼé a h-éaτaċ ʒaɲ ɼjaɲ ʒaɲ ċaɱ,
Ɗe'ɲ ʒ-cael aɲajɲτ ʒleʒejl ó ɲa h-Jɲɒjaċa aɲall,
Cael-baɲc ɼeaɲʒ ɼjoʒaɲɒa aʒ aɲ ċɲɲ Ɗja aɲ
ʒɲeaɲɲ,
Ɋ'ɼ ɒá ḃ-ɼejcɼeá aɲaʒajɒ aɲ lae j 'ɼ j aʒ éɲjʒeaɒ
aɼ ʒal!
Ɋ báɲ a láɲ, 7c.

III.

Ɋ Ḋaojlejɲ,* a ċɲojɲ-ċaɲɲajʒ ʒaɲḃ ʒaɲ ɼʒáċ,
Ɋjɲ aɲ ɲuaɒ-ḃaɲċ-ɼo ɼúɱ-ɼa bɼeaċɲɲʒ ɒo ɼáċ,
Ɋɲ ċɲɱjɲ leaτ, 'ɼ aɲ ʒ-cuaɲ-ɼo, ʒo ḃ-ɼaca τɼ báɒ
Ʒaɲ ċoɲτaḃajɲτ τoɲɲ-ḃaɲɲa ʒeaɲɲaɒ ɱaɲ τájɱ!
Ɋ báɲ a láɲ, 7c.

IV.

Ɋɼ cɲɱjɲ ljoɱ, a ɒuḃajɲτ Ḋaojleaɲ ʒuɲ caɲɲajʒ
ɱé ɒo ʒɲáċ,
'S ʒuɲ ab' ajɲ aɲ ʒ-cuaɲ ɼo jɼ bɼaɲ ɒaɱ aʒ aɱaɲċ
ʒaċ lá,
Ɋċ ɼljɲτeóʒ ɲj ċaḃaɲɼajɲ ajɲ a ḃ-ɼacaɼ ɒe bájɒ
Seaċ aɲ ɲuaɒ-ḃaɲc a'ɼa coɱplaċτ aʒ τaɲɲajɲʒ 'ɼ
aɲ τ-ɼɲáɲ!
Ɋ báɲ a láɲ, 7c.

*   *   *   *   *   *   *   *

* *Davilean*, a rock off Blacksod Bay.

II.

When draperied in her glorious trim of stainless dye,
The snow-white sails of canvas bleach'd 'neath India's
    sky,
Saw you her arrowy figure cleave the ocean vast,
GoD's favourite mounting on the wave before the
    blast !
          A flowing tide, &c.

III.

O, Dielion, tempest-beaten rock, all rough and dark,
Look forth, and see beneath me now this bounding
    bark,
And say, if e'er thou boat beheld within this bay,
Wave-mounted, cleaving, confident, like mine to-
    day !
          A flowing tide, &c.

IV.

Then answer'd ancient Dielion thus—"long ages o'er,
I've look'd abroad upon the bay that girds the
    shore—
But look'd in vain for boat or bark so swift and
    brave
As thine and all its gallant crew, to stem the wave!"
          A flowing tide, &c.

    *   *   *   *   *   *   *   *

V.

A aṫair na n-ḋúl, tabair ḋúinn-ne oiḋean na
  stáiġe,
Ġabaim do ċomairce rúd í a n-ïor an báḋ,
Tre ġarb ṫonntaib ṡobaḋaċ ṡá ċioċnar ġnáṫ,
A'r muna m-barraiḋ do ċuṁaċt ġaban rí trí mo
  lán!*

  A bán a lán, 7c.

——:o:——

SLÁN LE MÁIĠ.†

  An Manġaire Súġaċ, 7c.

I.

Slán a'r céaḋ óń t-taoḃro uaim,
Coir Máiġe na ġ-caor, na ġ-craoḃ, na ġ-cruaċ,
Na rtáiḋ, na reuḋ na raor, na rluaġ,
Na n-ḋán, na n-ḋreaċt, na ḋ-tréan ġan ġruaim!
  Oċ oċ óń! ir breoite mire,
  Ġan ċúḋ, ġan ċóir, ġan ċóir, ġan ċirte,
  Ġan rult, ġan reóḋ, ġan rpóirt, ġan rpionnaḋ
  O reólaḋ mé ċum uaiġnir!

II.

Slán ġo h-éaġ ḋa raór-ṡir ruairc,
Ḋa ḋáiṁ ḋá cléir, ḋá h-éiġr' ḋa ruaḋ,

---

* There is a want of strict connection between this stanza and
the preceding one. The intervening passages necessary to the
sense seem to have been lost.

V.

FATHER OF NATURE! how that boat comes dashing
    down,
Impetuous where the foamy surges darkly frown—
O! may THY mercy yield us now the sheltering
    shore,
Or yonder terror-stricken bark shall whelm us o'er!
        A flowing tide, &c.

—:o:—

FAREWELL TO THE MAIG.

I.

A long farewell I send to thee,
Fair Maig of corn and fruit and tree,
Of state and gift, and gathering grand,
Of song, romance, and chieftain bland.
    Uch, och ón! dark fortune's rigour—
    Wealth, title, tribe of glorious figure,
    Feast, gift—all gone, and gone my vigour,
    Since thus I wander lonely!

II.

Farewell for aye to the hearts I prize,
The poets, priests, and sages wise,

---

† The River Maig, in the County Limerick.

Ⱃom ċáɼⱱe cléɪƀ, ʒaɳ ċlaoɳ, ʒaɳ ċluaɪɳ,
Ʒaɳ ċáɪm, ʒaɳ ċaoɳ, ʒaɳ ċɼaoɼ ʒaɳ ċɼúaɼ!
    Oċ oċ óɳ, 7c.

III.

Sláɳ ⱱa éɪɼ ⱱá béɪċe uaɪɳɪ,
Ⱃa mɳáɪƀ ʒo léɪɼ, ⱱa ɼʒéɪɱ, ⱱa ɼɳuaⱱ,
Ⱃá ʒ-cáɪl, ⱱa ʒ-céɪl, ⱱa ʒ-caoɳ, ⱱa ʒ-cuaɪɳⱱ,
Ⱃa b-ɼɼáɼʒ, ⱱa b-pléɪⱱ, ⱱa méɪɳ, ⱱa m-buaⱱ!
    Oċ oċ óɳ, 7c.

IV.

Sláɳ ⱱaɼ aoɳ ⱱoɳ ⱱé ⱱaɼ ⱱual,
Uɳ báɪɳ-ċɳɪɼ béaɼaċ, béalⱱaɪɼ, buaⱱaċ,
Ċɳɼ ⱱɼáċ ċum ɼléɪƀ a ʒcéɪɳ am ɼuaɪʒ,
Sɪ ʒɼáⱱ mo cléɪƀ bɪ ɳéɪɼɪɳɳ ċuaɪⱱ!
    Oċ oċ óɳ, 7c.

V.

Jɼ ɼaʒɳaċ ɼaoɳ mé, ɪɼ ɼɳaoċɱaɼ, ɼuaɼ,
Jɼ ⱱaɪɱlaʒ, ⱱɼéɪċ, 'ɼ ɪɼ ⱱaoɱaċ, ⱱɼuaⱱ,
U m-baɼɼ aɳ ⱱɼléɪƀ ʒaɳ aoɳ, moɳuaɼ!
Um páɪɼⱱ aċⱱ ɼɳaoċ a'ɼ ʒaoċ a ⱱ-ⱱuaɪⱱ!
    Oċ oċ óɳ, 7c.

VI.

Ⱃoɳ ⱱ-ɼɼáɪⱱ 'ɳ uaɪɼ ċéɪʒɪm maɼ aoɳ aɪɼ cuaɪɼⱱ,
Nɪ h-áɪl leó mé, a'ɼ ɳɪ ɼeɪʒɪⱱ leaɼ clúaɪɳ,
Bɪⱱ mɳá le céɪle aʒ pléɪⱱ ⱱa luaⱱ,
Ca h-áɪⱱ? ca h-é? é ⱱaoƀ aɼ ʒluaɪɼ?
    Oċ oċ óɳ, 7c.

And bosom friends, whose boards display
Fair temperance blent with plenty gay !
Uch, och ón, &c.

III.

Farewell to the maids my memories bless,
To all the fair, to their comeliness,
Their sense, their fame, their mildness rare,
Their groups, their wit, their virtue fair !
Uch, och ón, &c.

IV.

Farewell to her to whom 'tis due,
The Fair-skin, gentle, mild-lipp'd, true,
For whom exil'd o'er the hills I go,
My heart's dear love, whate'er my woe !
Uch, och ón, &c.

V.

Cold, homeless, worn, forsaken, lone,
Sick, languid, faint, all comfort flown,
On the wild hill's height I'm hopeless cast,
To wail to the heath and the northern blast !
Uch, och ón, &c.

VI.

If through the crowded town I press,
Their mirth disturbs my loneliness;
And female groups will whisper—see !
Whence comes yon stranger ?—who is he ?
Uch, och ón, &c.

VII.

Dom cáirde am ġaoṙ-ġan teaċt is truaġ,
A's mé am ċráḋ ag an t-saoġal a ngéiḃ 'sa n-guais,
Le ráiṫe a b-péin a gcéin air cuairt
Gan áḃaċt, gan sgléip, gan sgéil da luaḋ!
Oċ oċ ón, 7c.

VIII.

O dáil an ċléir ḋam céile nuaḋ,
Cois Máige go h-eug ní h-é mo ċuairt,
Go bráṫ leam rae 'táim réiḋ leam ċuaċ,
Le mnáiḃ an t-saoġail ċrir mé air buairt.
Oċ oċ ón! mo ḃrón, mo ṁilleaḋ,
Iomarca an óil, a's póga brinneall,
Ċrir mise leam laeṫiḃ gan fód, gan foiṫin,
Fós gan iomad fuadair!

——:o:——

PLUR NA M-BAN DONN OG.*

I.

Dá d-tiocfa-sa liomsa go cŕntae liatroim;
A ṗlúr na m-ban donn óg,
Béarfainn-si mil beaċ agus méad mar ḃiaḋ ḋuit,
A ṗlúr na m-ban donn óg,

* *Plúna m-ban donn óg, Flower of brown-haired Maidens.* This beautiful song, which breathes the very soul of love and sorrow, seems to have been written at a period when famine afflicted the land. The poet's mistress declines, through dread of hunger, to

VII.

Thus **riven**, alas! from bosoms dear,
Amid dark danger, grief, and fear,
Three painful months unblest I rove,
Afar from friendship's voice and love!
Uch, och ón, &c.

VIII.

Forc'd by the priest, my love to flee,
Fair Maig through life I ne'er shall see;
And must my beauteous bird forego,
And all the sex that wrought me woe!
Uch och ón! my grief, my ruin!
'Twas drinking deep and beauty wooing
That caus'd, through life, my whole undoing,
And left me wandering lonely!

——:o:——

FLOWER OF BROWN-HAIRED MAIDENS.

I.

Oh! if thou come to Leitrim, sure nought can us
  sever,
      A phlur na m-ban donn óg!
Wild honey and the mead-cup shall feast us for ever,
      A phlur na m-ban donn óg!

visit with him the County of Leitrim, maugre all his glorious
painting; and he concludes his song with a burst of fierce love,
chastened down by grief and Christian resignation.

Ḃéaṙṙaṫ aeṙ ṅa loṅʒ ṅa ṙeól 'ṙ ṅa m-báṫ oṅʒ,
Ḟaoi ḃaṙṙaṫaiḃ ṅa ṫ-ṫom a'ṙ ṙiṅṅ aʒ ḟilleaṫ ó'ṅ
 ṫ-ṫṙáiʒ,
'Sṅi léiʒḟiṅṅ-ṙi aeṅ ḃṙón ċoiṫċe ṫo'ṫ ṫáil,
    A ṗlúṙ ṅa m-baṅ ṫoṅṅ óʒ!

II.

Ṅi ṙaċḟaiṫ miṙe leaʒ, a'ṙ ṅi'l maiṫ oṅʒ ṫo'm
 iaṙṙaiṫ,
    Ḋuḃaiṙʒ plúṙ ṅa m-baṅ ṫoṅṅ óʒ;
Waṙ ṅaċ ʒ-coiṅṅeóċaṫ ṫo ʒlóṙṫa beó ʒaṅ biaṫ mé,
    Ḋuḃaiṙʒ plúṙ ṅa m-baṅ ṫoṅṅ óʒ;
Wile céaṫ ḟeaṙṙ liom ḃeiṫ ċoiṫċe ʒaṅ ḟeaṙ,
Ná beiṫ aʒ ṙiuḃal aṅ ṫṙuċʒa 'ṙṅa ḃ-ḟáṙaċ leaʒ,
Ṅioṙ ṫuʒ mo ċṙoiṫe oṅʒ ʒṙáṫ ṅá ʒeaṅ,
    Ḋuḃaiṙʒ plúṙ ṅa m-baṅ ṫoṅṅ óʒ.

III.

Ċoṅaiṙc mé aʒ ʒeaċʒ ċuʒam i ʒṙé láṙ aṅ
 ʒ-ṙléiḃe,
    Waṙ ṙéilʒioṅ ʒṙiṫ aṅ ʒ-ceóṫ,
Ḃi mé aʒ caiṅʒ a'ṙ aʒ coṁṙáṫ léi
    ʒo ṅ-ṫeaċamaṙ ʒo páiṙc ṅa m-bó.
Ṡṙṫamaiṙṅe ṙioṙ a liḃ aṅ ḟáil,
ʒo ṫ-ʒuʒ mé ṫi ṙcṙioḃʒa ḟaoi mo láiṁ,
Ṅaċ ḃ-ḟṙil coiṙ ṫá ṅ-ṫéaṅaṫ ṙi ṅaċ ṅ-iocḟaiṅṅ a
 cáiṅ,
    Ḋo ṗlṙṙ ṅa m-baṅ ṫoṅṅ óʒ.

I'll show thee ships and sails, through the vistas
    grand,
As we seek our green retreat by the broad lake's
    strand,
And grief would never reach us within that happy
    land,
        A phlúr na m-ban donn óg !

II.

To Leitrim, to Leitrim, in vain thou would'st lead me,
        Duirt phlúr na m-ban donn óg.
When pale hunger comes, can thy melodies feed me ?
        Duirt phlúr na m-ban donn óg.
Sooner would I live, and sooner die a maid,
Than wander with thee through the dewy forest
    glade;
That thou art my beloved, this bosom never said,
        Duirt phlúr na m-ban donn óg.

III.

Over the mountain I once met the maiden,
        As a star through the mist might glow ;
We reach'd, while I told her my tale sorrow-laden,
        The field of the kine below ;
And there, in the hollow by the hedge-row tree,
I plighted her a promise, till life should flee,
To bear all the blame of her true love for me,
        Mo phlúr na m-ban donn óg.

D

IV.

Ⲁ̃o cⲣeⲁċ ⲁ'ⲣ mo cⲣáḋ ⳿ⳅⲁⲛ mé ꝼáⲓⲅⳅċe ⲅⲓoⲥ léⲓ,
Ⲁ̃o ṗlúⲣ ⲛⲁ m-bⲁⲛ ⲇoⲛⲛ óⳅ,
Ⲁⲓⲣ leⲁbⲁ ċⲁol áⲛⲇ, ⲛo ⲁⲓⲣ cáⲣⲛ ⲥ⳷be,
Ⲁ̃o ṗlúⲣ ⲛⲁ m-bⲁⲛ ⲇoⲛⲛ óⳅ,
Ⳬⲁⲛ ⲇⲩⲛe ⲁⲓⲣ bⲓ⳷ ⲁ ⲛ-eⲓⲣⲓⲛⲛ beⲓ⳷ láⲓ̃ liⲛⲛ 'ⲣⲁⲛ
oⲓ⳷ċe
Ⲁ̇ċⲥ ⲁⳅ ⲣúⳅⲛⲁḋ ⲁⳅⲩ ⲁⳅ ⳅáⲓⲛeⲁḋ ⲣéⲓⲛ mⲁⲣ bⲩḋ
m̃ⲁⲛⲛ liⲛⲛ,
Ⲁ Тhⲓⲁ, ⲛⲁċ cⲣⲩⲁḋ ⲁⲛ cáⲥ é mⲩⲛⲁ bꝼⲁⳅⲁⲓḋ mé ⲛⲓo
m̃ⲓⲁⲛⲛ,
Ⲁⲓⲣ ṗlúⲣ ⲛⲁ m-bⲁⲛ ⲇoⲛⲛ óⳅ.

—:o:—

Sⲓle Bheⲁⳅ Nⲓ Choⲓⲛⲇeⲁlbhⲁⲓⲛ.

I.

Ⲁ Shⲓle báⲛ ⲛⲁ b-ꝼeⲩⲣlⲁⲓḋe,
Ⲁ ċéⲁⲇ-ꝼeⲁⲛc ⲛáⲣ ꝼⲩllⲁⲓⳅ ⳅⲣⲩⲁⲓm,
Т'ꝼáⳅ ⲥú m'ⲓⲛ̃ⲥⲓⲛ bⲩⲁⲣⲥⲁ,
Ⲁ'ⲥ ⲁ'ⲇ ⲋⲓⲁⲓⲋⲅ̃ ⲛⲓ beⲓ⳷ mé bⲩⲁⲛ,
Ⲁ̃ⲩⲛⲁ ⲇ-ⲥⲓⳅⲓḋ ⲥú ⲇo'm ꝼeⲩċⲁⲓⲛ,
Ⲁ'ⲥ éⲩlóⳅⲁḋ lⲓom ꝼá ⳅleⲁⲛⲛⲥⲁⲓb cⲩⲁⲓⲛ,
Béⲓḋ cúm̃ⲁⲓḋ ⲁ'ⲥ ⲥⲩⲣⲥe ⲁ'ⲇ ⲋⲓⲁⲓḋ oⲣm,
Ⲁ'ⲥ béⲓḋ mé ċom̃ ⲇⲩb le ⳅⲩ́ⲁl.

II.

Ꞇⲩⳅⲥⲁⲣ ċⲩⳅⲁⲓ̃ ⲛⲁ ꝼⲓoⲛⲥⲁ,
Ⲁⳅⲩ lⲓoⲛⲥⲁⲣ ⲇⲩ́ⲛⲛ ⲁⲛ ⳅlⲁⲓⲛe ⲓⲥ ꝼeⲁⲣⲣ,
Ⲁ̃ⲩⲛⲁ b-ꝼⲁⳅⲁⲇ ꝼéⲓⲛ ceⲁⲇ ⲣⲓⲛⲥe,
le mⲓⲛ-ċⲛeⲓⲥ ⲁⲛ bⲣollⲁⲓċ báⲓⲛ;

IV.

Alas ! my sad heart, that I kiss not thy blushes,
    A phlúr na m-ban donn óg,
On a rich, lofty couch, or a heap of green rushes,
    Mo phlúr na m-ban donn óg.
Alone, all alone, through the beautiful night,
Laughing in the fulness of our hearts' delight ;
Alas ! if thou be not mine, how woful is my plight,
    A phlúr na m-ban donn óg !

——:o:——

LITTLE CELIA CONNELLAN.

I.

O ! pearl-deck'd, beauteous Celia,
    My first love of mildness rare !
My life full fast is fading,
    My soul is weary, vexed with care ;
Come, snowy-bosom'd maiden,
    And rove with me the valleys deep,
Or darkest gloom shall seize me,
    Till in the pitying grave I sleep !

II.

Come, place the cups before us,
    Let choicest wines their brims o'erflow—
We 'll drown, in draughts oblivious,
    The memory of her breast of snow ;

A plúr ir ȝile 'r ir mín̄e,
    Ná an ríoɒa 'r na clúm̄ na n-éan,
Ir buaiɒeanꞇa ꞇirreaċ bjóim̄re,
    'N uair rmuaníȝim bejꞇ rcarraṁr̄n léi.

III.

Ɒá m-bejóinn-ri féin a'r mín cneas,
    Caoin̄ean an brollaiċ breáȝ,
A n-ȝleannꞇán aoibin aereaċ,
    O ꞇr̄ꞇim ojóċe ȝo n-éir̄eóċaɒ lá,
Ȝan neaċ a bejꞇ ɒár ȝ-coin̄ɒeaċꞇ,
    Aċꞇ searca-fraojċ no 'n cojleaċ feaɒa,
'S ȝo m-bjaɒ ȝreann ȝan ċam am ċrojɒe rꞇiȝ,
    Ɒo Shile beaȝ ni' Choinɒealbáin!

------:o:------

A h-UISCIƊHE ĊROIƊHE NA N-ANAMAN.

I.

A h-uircjóe ċrojóe na n-anaman
    Leaȝan ꞇú air lár mé:
Bjóim ȝan ċéill ȝan ajꞇne,
    'Sé an ꞇ-eaċrann ɒo b'fearr liom;
Bjóeann mo ċóꞇa rꞇrácajóꞇe,
    Aȝur cailim leaꞇ mo ċarabaꞇ,
Ar bjoɒ a n-ɒearnair majꞇir̄e leaꞇ,
    Aċꞇ ꞇeanȝir̄ajɒ liom a máraċ!

Her neck, that's softer, fairer
    Than silk or plumes of snowy white ;
For memory wild pursues her
    When sever'd from my longing sight !

III.

Were thou and I, dear Smooth-neck !
    Of mild cheek and bosom white,
In a summer vale of sweetness
    Reposing through the beauteous night ; —
No living thing around us
    But heath-cocks wild till break of dawn,
And the sunlight of my bosom
    Were little Celia Connellan !

——:o:——

WHISKEY, SOUL OF REVELRY.

I.

THE POET.

Whiskey ! soul of revelry,
    Low in the mud you seat me—
Possess'd with all your devilry,
    I challenge foes to beat me—
Behold my coat to shreds is done,
    My neckcloth down the wind has run—
But I'll forgive the deeds you've done,
    If you to-morrow meet me !

II.

An uaiṗ éiṟoḟiḃ tuṟa an t-aiffṟionn,
    A'ṟ ḃéiḃ vo ṟailṁ ṗáṟóṫe,
Deunṟa ionao-coinne liom,
    A'ṟ teanzṁaiḃ liom a v-tiġ an táḃaiṗṗe,
Maṗ a ḃ-ḟeiciṟ cáiṗt a'ṟ cnazaiṗiḃ,
    A'ṟ coc a v-tóiṗ an ḃaṗṗaile,
A'ṟ bioḃ na h-aoiṗ a ṅ-aice leat,
    A'ṟ ṗoṁatṟa cṟṗḟeav ḟáilte.

III.

Oċ! mo ḟtóṗ azuṟ mo ċaṗa ṫú,
    Mo ṟiúṗ azuṟ mo ḃṗáṫaiṗ,
Mo ċṟiṗt, mo ṫiġ, mo ṫalaṁ ṫú,
    Mo ċṟuaċ, azuṟ mo ṟtáca,
Mo ṫṟeaḃaḃ ċéuċo, mo ċapaill ṫú,
    Mo ba 'ṟ mo ċaoiṗe zeala ṫú,
A'ṟ, ṫaṗ zaċ njḃ v'áṗ aiṗmṗiġeaṟ,
    Do ċonzḃaiḃ miṟe ṗáiṗt leat!

IV.

'Sa ṁṟṗṗiṗ ṁṟṗte ṁaṟzalaiċ,
    Jṟ taiṫneaṁaċ vo ṗóz liom,
Na viúltṟṗ ḟóṟ vo'm ċaṗṫaṗṗaċt,
    A'ṟ zuṗ ve'n ċineaḃ ċóiṗ mé,
Leañán-ṟiġe liom zin a'ṟ ṗum,
    Bṗáṫaiṗ zaoil vaṁ bṟaon te'n t-ṟult,
Jṟ caiṗveaṟ-Cṗioṟt vaṁ bowl o' punch,
    A'ṟ teanzṁaiḃ liom v'á ṫóṗṗḃeaċt!

II.

WHISKEY.

When after hearing Sunday mass,
  And your good psalm reciting,
Meet me at the wonted place,
  'Mid tavern joys delighting,
Where polish'd quarts are shining o'er
  The well-cock'd barrels on the floor,
And bring sweet rhymes, a goodly store,
  To grace my smiles inviting!

III.

BARD.

My store, my wealth, my cousin bland,
  My sister and my brother,
My court, my house, my farm of land,
  My stacks—I crave none other,
My labour, horses, and my plough,
  My white-fleec'd sheep, my cattle thou,
And far beyond all these I vow
  To love you as a mother!

IV.

Mild, beautiful, beloved one!
  Priz'd o'er all maids and misses!
O! quit me not, or I'm undone,
  My fathers lov'd your kisses—
My haunting sprite is rum, I trow;
  My blood relations, draughts that glow;
My gossip is the punch-bowl—O!
  I'll haste to share their blisses!

v.

Ir ıomṁóa bṗrıᵹın a'r eaċραηη,
    Bı eaṁραṁ lé ρáıτe,
Aċτ ηı ꜰαηαη bṗrón aṁ aıᵹηe,
    'Nuaır lıoηταρ ċúᵹaṁ aıρ cláρ τú,
Mo beaη aᵹur mo leaηb τú,
    Mo ṁáταıρ aᵹur mo aτaıρ τú,
Mo cóτa-móρ 'r mo ραρραρ τú,
    'S ηı rᵹαρꜰαıṁ mé ᵹo bṗáτ leaτ!

vi.

Τáıṁ ηa ᵹαolτa ır ꜰeaρρ aᵹαṁ,
    Da b-ꜰuıl a ṁ-τalaṁ Eıρeaη̃,
leaηη a'r bṗaηṁa a'r uırce-beaṫa,
    Aċτ ηaċ τ-ταᵹαηη aη claραéıṁ lıom,
Bṗoηηαım rúṁ ṁo'η Eaᵹlır,
    Maρ ır móρ mo ṛl aρ a m-beaηηnᵹτcaċτ,
A'r ᵹuρ maıτ leó bṗaoη ṁo blaıρeaṁ ṫe,
    Ḋ'éır aıꜰrıηη ṁo léuᵹaṁ ṁṛηη!

——:o:——

PAISTIN FIONN.*

i.

Ꞡráṁ le m-aηαṁ mo Pháırτıη Fıoηη,
A cρoıṁe 'r a h-aıᵹηe aᵹ ᵹáıρıṁ lıom,
A cıoċa ᵹeala maρ bláτ ηa η-úball,
'Ꞡa ρıob maρ eala lá Mápτa!

* *Paistin Fionn, the Fair Young Child.*

v.

What quarrels dire we both have had
   This year of sorrow sable!
But O! my bounding heart is glad
   To see you crown the table—
Dear fondling of the nuptial nest,
   My father kind, my mother blest,
My upper coat, my inner vest,
   I'll hold you while I'm able!

vi.

The friends, the very best I saw,
   While through the land a rover,
Were brandy, ale, and usquebaugh—
   Of claret I'm no lover;
That liquor may the clergy bless—
   Though great I deem their holiness,
They like the claret ne'ertheless,
   When Mass and psalm are over!

———:o:———

THE FAIR YOUNG CHILD.

i.

My *Paistin Fionn* is my soul's delight—
Her heart laughs out in her blue eyes bright;
The bloom of the apple her bosom white,
   Her neck like the March swan's in whiteness!

Cúṁ ḟa.

Jr ṫura mo rún, mo rún, mo rún,
Jr ṫura mo rún a'r mo ġráḋ ġeal,
Jr ṫura mo rún, a'r mo ċoṁan ġo buan,
'Sé mo ċreaċ ġan tú aġam ó'ḋ ṁáṫairín!

II.

Cara mo ċroiḋe mo Pháirtín Fionn,
B-ḟuil a ḋá ġnuaḋ air laraḋ mar bláṫ na ġ cnann,
Tá mire raen air mo Ṗáirtín Fionn,
Aċt aṁáin ġur ólar a rláinte!
Cúṁ ḟa.
Jr ṫura mo rún, mo rún, mo rún, 7c.

III.

Dá m-beiḋinnri annra m-baile m-biaḋ ruġraḋ a'r
ġneann,
No ioin ḋá ḃarraile lán te leann;
Mo ṫírín a'm aici 'r mo láṁ faoi na ceann,
Jr rúġaċ ḋo ólfain a rláinte!
Cúṁ ḟa.
Jr ṫura mo rún, mo rún, mo rún, 7c.

IV.

Ḃí mé naoi n-oiḋċe a'm luiḋe ġo boċt,
O beiṫ rínte faoi an ḋilinn ioin ḋá ṫop,
A ċomainn mo ċroiḋe, a'r mé aġ rmuaineaḋ ort,
'S naċ b-faġaṁri le feaḋ 'ná le ġlaoḋ tú!
Cúṁ ḟa.
Jr ṫura mo rún, mo rún, mo rún, 7c.

CHORUS.

O! you are my dear, my dear, my dear,
  O! you are my dear, and my fair love ;
You are my own dear, and my fondest hope here ;
  And O! that my cottage you'd share, love!

II.

Love of my bosom, my fair Páistín,
Whose cheek is red like the rose's sheen ;
My thoughts of the maiden are pure, I ween,
  Save toasting her health in my lightness !
  O! you are my dear, my dear, &c.

III.

Were I in our village where sports prevail,
Between two barrels of brave brown ale,
My fair little sister to list my tale,
  How jovial and happy I'd make me !
  O! you are my dear, my dear, &c.

IV.

In fever for nine long nights I've lain
From lying in the hedge-row beneath the rain,
While, gift of my bosom ! I hop'd in vain
  Some whistle or call might awake ye !
  O! you are my dear, my dear, &c.

v.

Tréigfeaḋ mo ċairaiḋ 'r mo ċáirḋe gaoil,
A'r tréigfiḋ mé a mairean ḋe ṅináiḃ a t-raoġail,
Ní tréigfeaḋ le'm ṁarċainn tú, gráḋ mo ċroiḋe,
Go rinfear a g-cóiṁra faoi clár mé!

Curr fa.

Ir tura mo rún, mo rún, mo rún,
Ir tura mo rún, a'r mo gráḋ geal,
Ir tura mo rún, a'r mo ċoman go buan,
'Sé mo ċreaċ gan tú agam ó'ḋ ṁáċairín!

——:o:——

AN SEOTḢO.*

Eoġan Ruaḋ, ró ċán.

I.

Seotó ṫoil! ná goil go fóil,
Ḋo ġeaḃair gan ḋearmaḋ a ḋ-tairge gaċ reóiḋ
Ḋo bí ag aḋ rinrean ríogṫa nómaḋ,
An Eirinn iaṫ-ġlair ċrinn a'r Eoġan!
    Seotó ṫoil, ná goil go fóil,
    Seotó leinḃ, a ċumainn 'ra rtóirr,
    Mo ċúig ċéaḋ ċúṁaḋ go ḋúbaċ faoi ḃrón,
    Tu ag rile 'na rúl a'r ḋo cóṁ gan lón!

* The *Seotho*, or *Lullaby*, was the extempore effusion of Owen Roe O'Sullivan, to soothe the infantile sorrows of an illegitimate child, which one of the victims of his illicit amours had left him. Owen's patience and promises, it is said, were nearly exhausted.

v.

From kinsfolk and friends, my fair, I'd flee,
And all the beautiful maids that be,
But never I'll leave sweet *gradh mo chroidhe,*†
Till death in your service o'ertake me!

CHORUS.

O! you are my dear, my dear, my dear,
   O! you are my dear, and my fair love;
You are my own dear, and my fondest hope here;
   And O! that my cottage you'd share, love!

——:o:——

THE LULLABY.

I.

Hush, baby mine, and weep no more,
Each gem thy regal fathers wore,
When Erin, Emerald Isle, was free,
Thy poet sire bequeaths to thee!
      Hush, baby dear, and weep no more;
      Hush, baby mine, my treasur'd store;
      My heart-wrung sigh, my grief, my groan,
      Thy tearful eye, thy hunger's moan!

when the unfortunate mother, urged by maternal feelings, again
returned to claim the child.
   † *Gradh mo Chroidhe, Love of my Heart.* The Irish is to be
pronounced as if written *Gra mu cree.*

II.

Ɗo ʒeabaɲ aɲ ꝺ-ꞇꞃ́ꞃ aɲ ꞇ'ubal aꝺ ꝺóɪꝺ,
Ɗo bɪ aʒ aɲ ꝺ-ꞇꞃɪꞃ́ɲ a ʒ-clꞃ́ꝺ ꞅaoɪ coɲɱéaꝺ ;
Aɲ ꞃꞇaꝼ ꝺo bɪ aʒ Paɲ ba ʒꞃeaɲꞇa 'ɲ ꞇ-ꞃeóɪꝺ,
'S aɲ ꞇ·ꞃlaꞇ ꝺo bɪ aʒ Ɯaoɪꞃ ʒɲɪoꝺ ꝺɪoɲ ꝺó 'ꞅ
ꞇꞃeoɪɲ !

Seoꞇó ꞇoɪl, ꞏc.

III.

Ɗo ʒeabaɲ aɲ caol eac éaꝺꞇꞃom óʒ,
Ɗo ʒeabaɲ aɲ ꞃꞃɪaɲ 'ꞅ aɲ ꝺɪallaɪꞇ óɪꞃ,
Bɪ aʒ Ꝼaɪlꞇ̃e Ꝼɪoɲɲ ba ꞇeaɲ aɲ ꞇóɪꞃ,
Uʒ ꞃuaʒaꝺ Ɗaɲ̃aɲ ó Chaɪꞃeal ʒo Bóɲ̃ɲ.

Seoꞇó ꞇoɪl, ꞏc.

IV.

Ɗo ʒeabaɲ cloɪꝺeaɱ ꞃolɲꞃ aɲ ꝺoꞃɲ-cꞃ̃l óɪꞃ
Ɗo bɪ aʒ Bꞃɪaɲ aʒ ɲɪaɲ ɲa ꞅluaʒa,
Aɲ boʒa bɪ aʒ Ɯuꞃcaꝺ aɲ uꞃcaɲ ɱóɪꞃ,
Uʒ caꞇ Cluaɲ-Ꞇaɲꞇ̃ aʒ ꞇꞃeaꞃʒaꞃ ɲa ꝺ-ꞇꞃeoɪɲ !

Seoꞇó ꞇoɪl, ꞏc.

V.

Uꞃꝺ-cꞃ̃ 'ɲ ꞇaɪꞃꝺɪl ó Caɪꞃeal ɲa ɲ-óꞃꝺ,
O leoʒaɲ ꝼaɪꞇce Buɲ-Raɪꞇe ɲa ꞃeól,
Jolaɲ ꞃléɪꞇ̃e, caol cꞃoɪꞇ ceoɪl,
'S ꞃeabac ɲa ꞃeɪlʒ ó Sʒeɪlʒ ɲa ꞃʒeól.

Seoꞇó ꞇoɪl, ꞏc.

VI.

Ɗo ʒeabaɲ lomꞃaꝺ ꞃaɪꝺbɪꞃ aɲ óɪꞃ,
Ꞇhuʒ Jaꞃoɲ ꞇꞃéaɲ ꝺo'ɲ Ʒhꞃéɪʒ aɪꞃ bóꞃꝺ ;

II.

I'll give the fruit the Phrygian boy
Bestow'd on Venus, queen of joy—
The staff of Pan, the shepherd's God,
And Moses' wonder-working rod.
    Hush, baby dear, &c.

III.

The steed of golden housings rare,
Bestrode by glorious Falvey Fair,
The chief who at the Boyne did shroud,
In bloody wave, the sea-kings proud !
    Hush, baby dear, &c.

IV.

Brian's golden-hilted sword of light,
That flash'd despair on foeman's flight ;
And Murcha's fierce, far-shooting bow,
That at Clontarf laid heroes low !
    Hush, baby dear, &c.

V.

The courier hound that tidings bore
From Cashel to Bunratty's shore ;
An eagle fierce, a bird of song,
And Skellig's hawk, the fierce and strong.
    Hush, baby dear, &c.

VI.

I'll give, besides, the golden fleece
That Jason bore to glorious Greece ;

'San τρaη-eaċ cuṫaιʒ, meaη, cumaτaċ óʒ,
Bí aʒ Cuċullaιη ceaηη-uηηaṫ ηa rluaʒ.
        Seoṫó ṫoιl, 7c.

VII.

Do ʒeabaιη rιcaʒa Aιcιll ba ċalma a η-ʒleó,
'S cρaoιreaċ Fιηη ʒaη ṁoιll aτ ṫóιτ;
Eιτe Conηaιl τo b-uηηaṫ le τρeoη,
'S rʒιaṫ ʒeal Naoιr ó cρaoιb ηa rluaʒa.
        Seoṫó ṫoιl, 7c.

VIII.

Do ʒeabaιη cloιṫeaṁ Fιηη ba ljoṁṫa a η-ʒleó,
'S aη ʒaṫ bí aʒ Dιaρmuιτ τριaṫ ηa leóʒaη,
Cloʒaτ cuρaητa Orʒuιη ṁóιη,
Aιη faιṫċe ηa féιηηe τρaoċ Mac Τρeóιη.
        Seoṫó ṫoιl, 7c.

IX.

Do ʒeabaιη a leιηb maη ṫγlle leó aη τ-reóιτ,
Τhuʒ Aoιfe τ'éιr ʒaċ céιm τo'η leóʒaη,
Le'η ṁaηb Feaητιaṫa ba ṫιaη a τ-τóιη,
'S Coηlaoċ uaral, uaιbρeaċ óʒ!
        Seoṫó ṫoιl, 7c.

X.

Do ʒeabaιη ʒaη ṁeaηball faηηaιṫ ʒaċ reoιτ,
Dιoη bρaτ τubρaṫ Dúblaιηʒ óιʒ,
Do ċeιleaṫ a ʒηγ́r a ʒcóṁʒηac rluaʒ,
'S é aʒ rιoη-ċuη laoċ ʒo faoη ṫá τ-τρeoιη.
        Seoṫó ṫoιl, 7c.

The harp-sung steed that history boasts,
Cuchullin's—mighty chief of hosts!
   Hush, baby dear, &c.

VII.

His spear who wrought great Hector's fall,
The mighty javelin of Fingal;
The coat of mail that Connal wore,
The shield that Naois in battle bore.
   Hush, baby dear, &c.

VIII.

Fingal's swift sword of death and fear,
And Diarmid's host-compelling spear;
The helm that guarded Oscar's head,
When fierce Mac Treon beneath him bled.
   Hush, baby dear, &c.

IX.

Son of old chiefs! to thee is due
The gift Aoife gave her champion true,
That seal'd for aye Ferdia's doom,
And gave young Conlaoch to the tomb.
   Hush, baby dear, &c.

X.

Nor shall it be ungiven, unsung,
The mantle dark of Dulaing young,
That viewless left the chief who laid
Whole hosts beneath his batttle blade!
   Hush, baby dear, &c.

XI.

Ɗo ʒeabaın ríoʒan ṁın ⫶aır, ṁoⅾaṁaıl,
Jr áılne ʒnaoı, 'r ır caoıne rnuaⅾa,
Ná 'n péılⸯıon ʒrínn ⫶uʒ Prıam 'r a ŕluaʒa,
Ɉo bán na Ⱶráoı ʒan ⫶ím ʒan ⫶reóın.
Seoⱬó ⫶oıl, 7c.

XII.

Ɗo ʒeabaın nıⱶ nán ṁṅⅾear onⱬ fór,
Ɉloıne ⱬo'n ŕıon bıⱬ bnıoʒṁan roⅾaṁṅıl,
Ɗo ⱬannaınʒeaⱬ ḣebe, an péılⸯıon óʒ,
Cḣuṁ Jupıⸯen Laoⱬ na n-ⅾéıⱬe aın bónⅾ.
Seoⱬó ⫶oıl, 7c.

XIII.

Ɗo ʒeabaın ⫶ṅlle nan ṁṅríⅾear fór,
Ⱥn ʒaⱬ ⱬuʒ Ⱥonʒur ⫶éan 'na ⱬóıⅾ,
Ɗo ṁac calṁa Uı Ɗhṅbne ⱬá ⫶íon aın ⫶óın,
Ⱳan ba mınıc an Fhıann ʒo ⅾıan 'na ⅾeⱬⱬaıʒ.
Seoⱬó ⫶oıl, 7c.

XIV.

Ɗo ʒeabaın raıll uaın fíon a'r beoın,[*]
Ⱥ'r éaⅾaⱬ 'na naıce ba ṁaıre ⱬo ⫶reoın,
Ⱥⱬ ó ⱬím ⅾo ṁṅṁe ⱬúʒam ran nóⅾ,
Nı ʒeallfaⅾ uaın ⱬṅⱬ ⅾuaır ná reóıⅾ !
Seoⱬó ⫶oıl, ná ʒoıl ʒo fóıl !
Seoⱬó leınb, a cuṁaınn 'ra rⱬóın,
Ⱳo cúıʒ céaⅾ cuṁaⱬ ʒo ⅾúbaⱬ faoı brón,
Ⱶu aʒ rıle 'na rúl a'r ⅾo cóṁ ʒan lón !

---

[*] *Beoir* was a delicious liquor, anciently made from mountain heath. Tradition asserts that the Danes alone possessed the secret

XI.

And eke a maid of modest mien,
Of charms beyond the Spartan queen,
Whose awful, soul-subduing charms
Mov'd Priam to dare a world in arms!
Hush, baby dear, &c.

XII.

For thee shall sparkle, in my lays,
Rich nectar from young Hebé's vase,
Who fill'd the cup in heaven's abodes,
For Jove, amid the feast of Gods.
Hush, baby dear, &c.

XIII.

Another boon shall grace thy hand,
Mac Duivne's life-protecting brand,
Great Aongus' gift, when Fenian foe
Pursu'd his path with shaft and bow!
Hush, baby dear, &c.

XIV.

And dainty rich, and *beoir* I'll bring,
And raiment meet for chief and king;
But gift and song shall yield to joy—
Thy mother comes to greet her boy!
Hush, baby dear, and weep no more;
Hush, baby mine, my treasur'd store;
My heart-wrung sigh, my grief, my groan,
Thy tearful eye, thy hunger's moan!

of preparing it, and also that for this purpose they divided the heathy tracts among them, in preference to the arable land.

NEILLIƊE BÁN.

I.

A Neilljƌe Bháṅ rúƌ láiṁ liom a ċaraƌ ġeal mo
ċroiƌe,

Ar léiġ mo láiṁ air ƌo ḃráġaiƌ nó ní ṁairfe mé
beó miƌe,

Ɗo ṡnáiṁfiṅ an tSruiḃ aġus an tSionaiṅ ġeal aƌ
ƌiaiġ,

A'r ġur nuaġ tu bárr leat ó ṁnáiḃ ḃreáġa baile
loċa Riaċ.*

II.

Ɗa mo leamra Portumna 'ġur baile loċa Riaċ,

Luimneaċ na long aġus conntae Bhaile aċ Cliaṫ,†

Air ƌo ṁúintir ƌo roiṅfinre a leaṫ aġus a
ƌ-trian,

Ɗo foṅ ƌul a ccleaṁnar leat lá faƌa 'r bliaṫain.

III.

Beir mo ḃeaṅaċtra ġo Connaċta mar ar aṅ ƌo ḃí
an ġreaṅ,

A'r ġo ƌtí mo ḃalaintín ar faƌa tá rí uaim;

An t-ionaƌ coiṅe úƌ ḃí eaƌraiṅ aġ rléiḃte ƌúba
Tuaƌṁuṁan

A rí an t-Sionaiṅ ġeal ƌo ċoinġiḃ me ḃí lán ġo
bruaċ.

---

* *Baile-loch-readhach,* the town of Loughrea, on the lake of
the same name, in the County Galway.

† *Baile-ath-cliath,* the Irish name for the city of Dublin. Our

NELLY BAN.

I.

O, sit beside me, Nelly Bán, bright favourite of my
  heart,
Unless I touch thy snowy neck my life will soon
  depart—
I'd swim for thee the River Suir and Shannon's
  widespread sea:
Thou dost excel the beauteous maids of the town on
  blue Loch Rea!

II.

Were mine the town on blue Loch Rea, Portumna's
  pleasant streets,
The city of the Battle-ford, and Limerick of the
  fleets,
Unto thy tribe these precious gifts I gladly would
  resign,
Could gifts like these incline them, love, to make thee
  ever mine!

III.

My blessing take to Connaught back, the land of
  friendship free,
And to my own beloved who is so far from me;
On Thomond's dusky mountain, our meeting-place
  we chose—
Swoln Shannon's waves detain'd me—in savage wrath
  they rose!

historians say that *Baile-ath-cliath* literally means the *Town of the
ford of hurdles*; but as *cliath* might mean either a *hurdle* or a *battle*,
I have chosen the latter version as better suited to my verse.

IV.

Ɖob ḟeáɲ l̩oɱ ná ɱo ċapall aɲ ʒaɲ áɲɲoɩɲ a
ṙɲɩaɲ,

21'ɲ ná ḟáḃalṭaɲ ɲa páɩɲce ɩoɲa leaʒṭaɲ ɲa
ꝼɩaḋa ;

'Ná ṭṭáɩɲɩc ꝺe ḃáꝺaɩḃ ó Bhaɩle aṫ Clɩaṫ ʒo
Lɩ̩ɱꝑeaċ le blɩaḋaɩɲ,

Ná ꝼaɩcꝼɩɲ ṭuɲa a ʒɲáꝺ ʒɩl aɲ ṙɲáɩꝺ Baɩle loċa
Rɩaċ.

V.

Ɖob ḟeáɲ l̩oɱ ʒo ɱbeɩꝺíɲ ɱaɲḃ aʒuɲ ɲíɲṭe aɲ
aɲ ṭ-ɲl̩aḃ,

2Ꝺo láɱ ṫeaɲ anáɩɲꝺe ꝺá ꝑɩoca aʒ aɲ ḃꝼɩaċ!

21 ɲꝺáɲ ʒuɲ ṫɲ̩ṭ ɱé a ɲʒɲáꝺ leaṭ a Neɩllɩꝺe
Ḃáɲ ɲa cclɩaɱ,

21'ɲ ʒo ɲꝺeɩɲ ꝺo ɱáṭaɩɲíɲ ɲaċ áɩl léɩ ɱɩɲe ꝺɩ̩ṭ
ɱaɲ clɩaɱ̩ɲ̩ɲ.

——:o:——

'Be N-Eɩrɩnn ɩ.*

Uɩllɩaɱ Ɖall, ɲó ċáɲ.

I.

21 n-ʒleanṭaɩḃ ɲéɩɲ ɲa h-éɩʒɲe bɩɱ,

21 ḃ-ꝼanɲṭaɩꝛ péɩnɲ a n-ʒéɩḃ ʒaċ laoɩ ;

21n ṭ-ɲeanʒ-bean ʒle ba béaɲaċ ʒɲaoɩ

Ɖo ɲʒannɲaɩꝺ ɱé, 'bé ɲ-Eɩɲɩnn í!

'Bé ɲ-Eɩɲɩnn í!

* 'Be n-Eirinn i, literally means *Whoever she be in Ireland.*

IV.

I would sooner than my gallant steed—I pass his
  bridle-rein,
Or heirdom of the wide domain where stately deer
  are slain;
Than all that reach'd to Limerick of laden fleets this
  year,
That in the town on blue Loch Rea I could behold
  my dear!

V.

O! that I were laid in death far on a hill away,
My right hand high extended to feed the bird of
 • prey,
Since, Nelly Bán, the theme of bards, I fell in love
  with thee,
And thy mother says she'll have me not, her son-in-
  law to be!

——:o:——

'BE N-EIRINN I.

I.

In Druid vale alone I lay,
Oppress'd with care, to weep the day—
My death I ow'd one sylph-like she,
Of witchery rare, *'be n-Eirinn i!*
      'Be n-Eirinn i!

II.

Ní tʆácʆa mé aιʆ céιle Naoιʆ
Thus áʆ na n-ʒaoιʆeal aιʆ ʆ-ʆeacʆ ʆon Chʆιaoιʃ,
Na an ʃáʃ ʆ'n n-ʒʆéιʒ ʆo céaʆ an Tʆaoι,
Le ʒʆáʆ mo cléιʃ, 'ʃé n-ʆιʆιnn ι!
'Bé n-ʆιʆιnn ι!

III.

'S ʃʆeáʒa ʆeaʆ ʆʆéιmʆeaʒ ʆéιʆ a ʆlaoι,
ʒo ʃáʆʆ an ʆéιʆ na ʆlaoʆ aιʆ ʃιʒ,
A ʆláʆ-ʆolʆ ʆéιʒ ʆo ʆealʆaʆ an ʆlιoʆ,
Aιʆ ʒʆáʆ mo cléιʃ, 'ʃé n-ʆιʆιnn ι!
'Bé n-ʆιʆιnn ι!

IV.

Iʆ cáʆʃaʆ, ʆaoʆac ʆeuʆac ʃιʆιm,
ʒo cʆáιʆʆe, cʆeιmeac, ceuʆʆa ʆ'n mʆáoι,
Faʒnac, ʆáon, ʒan céιll, aιʆ ʃaoιʆ,
Le ʒʆáʆ ʆo'n ʃéιʆ, 'ʃé n-ʆιʆιnn ι!
'Bé n-ʆιʆιnn ι!

V.

Aιʆ neóιn n-uaιʆ ʆéιʒιm aιʆ ʆaoʃ ʆʆʒe Fιnn,
Fa ʃʆón a ʒcéιn a'ʆ ʒan aón ʆam ʃʆʆóιn,
Cιa ʆeolʆaʆ aon Whac ʆé am lιon
Aʆ ʆʆóʆ mo cléιʃ, 'ʃé n-ʆιʆιnn ι!
'Bé n-ʆιʆιnn ι!

II.

The spouse of Naisi, Erin's woe—
The dame that laid proud Ilium low,
Their charms would fade, their fame would flee,
Match'd with my fair, *'be n-Eirinn i!*
    'Be n-Eirinn i!

III.

Behold her tresses, unconfin'd,
In wanton ringlets woo the wind,
Or sweep the sparkling dew-drops free,
My heart's dear maid, *'be n-Eirinn i!*
    'Be n-Eirinn i!

IV.

Fierce passion's slave, from hope exil'd,
Weak, wounded, weary, woful, wild—
Some magic spell she wove for me,
That peerless maid, *'be n-Eirinn i!*
    'Be n-Eirinn i!

V.

But O! one noon I clomb a hill,
To sigh alone—to weep my fill,
And there Heaven's mercy brought to me
My treasure rare, *'be n-Eirinn i!*
    'Be n-Eirinn i!

CAITILIN NI UALLACHAIN.*

Uilliam Dall, ró cán.

I.

Ir faða mílte ðá ccantað ríor 'r ruar an fázan,
A'r claña raoiðe an earbaið zniñ zan cluain, zan
    rðáiɼ ;
Zan cánað laoi, zan fleaza, zan fion, zan cnuar,
    zan ceánð,
Aɼ bnaið aníɼ aɼ Caitilín ni Uallacáin !

II.

Ná mearaiziðe zun caile ćnion na zuaineacán,
Na caillicín an ainfin mín-ðair, buacać, mnáñil ;
Ir faða aníɼ ba banalðna í, 'r ba mór a h-áðal,
Ða mbeiðeað acð an Rí̃z az Caitilín ni Uallacáin !

III.

Ba ðear a znaoi ðá mainimíɼ le nuazað náñað,
Bnaða ríoða az ðannɼnz zaoiðe 'r buað ćun bab ;
Plaið zo znóiðe ó baðar cín anuar zo ðnáćð
Az mac an Rí̃z ain Chaitilín ni Uallacáin !

* In this political poem, composed by blind William Heffernan,
commonly called *Uilliam Dall,* Ireland is personified under the

CAITILIN NI UALLACHAN.

I.

How sad our fate, driven desolate o'er moor and
    wild,
And lord and chief, in gloom and grief, from home
    exil'd,
Of songs divine, and feasts and wine, and science
    lorn,
We pine unseen for *Caitilin ni Uallachán.*

II.

Suppose not now that wrinkled brow, or unkempt
    hair,
Or long years' rigour did e'er disfigure the queenly
    Fair—
Her numerous Race would find their place on Erin's
    lawn,
If the prince had been with his *Caitilin ni Uallachán.*

III.

Fair were her cheek could we live to wreak the foe-
    man's rout,
And flags would gleam to the breeze's stream o'er
    victory's shout ;
And richest plaid on the happy maid may trail the
    lawn,
If the prince had been with his *Caitilin ni Uallachán!*

name of *Caitilín ni Uallachán,* or *Catharine ó Houlihan.*

IV.

Sᴣпeaᴅaᴍaoﾌᴅ le ɦ-aⱦċꞃñﾌⱦe ċuᴍ uaꞃ ꞃa ꞃᴣпáɼ,
Ɖo ċeap ꞃa Ꞇﾌoɼⱦa, ⱦalaꞃ ⱦﾌɼﾌᴍ, 'ɼ cɼuaċaﾌɓ
áпᴅ ;
Ɖo ɼᴣaﾌp ꞃa ⱦⱦﾌᴍpċﾌoll ꝼaﾌꞃᴣﾌⱦe, ᴣeal-ċuaꞃⱦa 'ɼ
ⱦɼáﾌᴣ,
Aᴣ cuɼ ᴍalaﾌɼⱦ cɼﾌċe aɼ Chaﾌⱦﾌlﾌꞃ ꞃﾌ Ullaċáﾌꞃ !

V.

Aꞃ ⱦé ⱦaɼпꞃꞃᴣ Jɼпael ⱦɼeaɼ ꞃa ⱦaoﾌᴅe Ruaᴅ ó
ꞃáᴍꞃᴅ,
Ɖo ɓeaⱦaﾌᴅ ᴅaoﾌꞃe ᴅaⱦaᴅ ᴣéﾌᴍпﾌᴅ aꞃuaɼ le
ɦ-aпáꞃ ;
Ɖo ꞃeaɼⱦaﾌᴅ Ꝏaoﾌɼ a ᴍeaɼᴣ a ꞃáᴍaﾌᴅe, ꝼuaɼᴣaﾌl,
ⱦɼáﾌⱦ,
Jɼ ⱦaɓaﾌɼ ᴅﾌoꞃ ᴅo Chaﾌⱦﾌlﾌꞃ ꞃﾌ Uallaċáﾌꞃ !

——:o:——

A ShﾌOBhAN A RUﾌN.*

I.

A Shﾌoɓáꞃ a Rꞃ́ꞃ, ﾌɼ ⱦú ᴅo ᴍaɼɓ ᴍe пﾌaᴍ,
A Shﾌoɓáꞃ a Rꞃ́ꞃ, ﾌɼ ⱦú ᴅo ɓaﾌꞃ ᴅﾌoᴍ ᴍo ċﾌall,
A Shﾌoɓáꞃ a Rꞃ́ꞃ, ﾌɼ ⱦú ċúaᴅaﾌɼ eaᴅaɼ ᴍe a'ɼ Ɖﾌa,
A'ɼ ɓ-ꝼeáɼɼ ᴅꞃ́ꞃꞃe ɓeﾌⱦ ᴣaꞃ ɼꞃ́lﾌɓ ꞃa ⱦú ꝼeﾌcɼﾌꞃ
aɼﾌaᴍ !

* I found these fugitive lines untranslated in Hardiman's
" Minstrelsy," and have taken the liberty of transferring them
hither, and giving them an English dress, which they very richly

IV.

We raise our eye with suppliant cry to the Lamb of
    Grace
Who form'd the tide—did the lands divide—gave hills
    their place—
Who spread around the seas profound, and bay, and
    lawn—
To change the scene for *Caitilin ni Uallachán!*

V.

Who Israel led where the Red Sea sped its waves of
    fear,
His table spread with Heaven's blest bread for forty
    year,
In favouring hour gave Moses power and freedom's
    dawn,
Shall come to screen his *Caitilin ni Uallachán!*

——:o:——

O, JUDITH, MY DEAR.

I.

O, Judith, my dear, 'tis thou that hast left me for
    dead ;
O, Judith, my dear, thou'st stolen all the brain in my
    head ;
O, Judith, my dear, thou'st cross'd between Heaven
    and me,
And 'twere better be blind than ever thy beauty to see!

deserve. *Siobhan* is Anglicised *Judith* by the Scotch, and Johauua
by the Irish.

II.

Ar breáʒ é ꞇo ṙnoꞇ, ır ꞇú aɲ ꞇ-reóıꞇ ꞇo cuɱaꞇ
ʒo ceapꞇ ;
Jr ꞇú 'ɲ caılıɲ óʒ ɲaċ paıb ólꞇaċ, ıɱırꞇeaċ leaɱ ;
Do ʒruaꞇ ɱaɲ aɲ róʀ a'r ꞇo póʒ ɱaɲ ṙılleaꞇ ɲa
ɱ-beaċ,
A'r ʒuɲ é ꞇo ċeól ɲéıꞇ ċuʒ ɱé ó ċıɲɲeaꞇ a
ṙeaɲc !

——:o:——

AJSLJNʒ ŚEAʒAJN AꞂhJC ꝊOAꞂhNAJLL.*

I.

Oıꞇċe bíoꞇ aɱ lıʒe aɱ ṙuaɲ,
'S ɱé aıɲ buaıɲeaꞇ ꞇɲé ɲa caċaıʒe ;
Do ṙıɲ aɲ ꞇṙıꞇ-beaɲ, ꞇṙıꞇleaċ, ꞇruaıɲc,
Taob lıoɱ ruaʀ aʒ ꞇéaɲaıɲ ꞇaċaıʒe :
Ba ċaol a cóɱ, a cɲaob-ṙolꞇ ꞇɲóɱ,
Aʒ ꞇeaċꞇ ʒo boṅ léı ɲa ꞇɲaċaıʒe,
Ba ꞇȟbe a ʒɲuaıʒ 'ɲá aɲ ʒual,
'S ba ʒıle a ʒɲuaꞇ 'ɲá ɲa h-Allaıꞇe.

II.

Do ċoɲaɲc í, ʒɲaoı ʒaɲ ʒɲuaıɱ,
A claoɲ-poırʒ uaıꞇɲe 'ra béal ꞇaɲaıʒe ;
A ɱıoɲ ċıoċ, cɲȟɲ, ʒeal, cɲuaıꞇ,
Aıɲ a ɱıɲ-ċɲeır ṙuaɲ ɲaċ bṙȟl ꞇcaꞇaıʒe ;

* This allegorical poem, in which the genius of Ireland, imper-
sonated by a queen of Faëry, leads the charmed mortal through the

II.

Thy person is peerless—a jewel full fashion'd with care,

Thou art the mild maiden so modest at market and fair,

With cheek like the rose, and kiss like the store o' the bee,

And musical tones that call'd me from death unto thee !

——:o:——

THE VISION OF JOHN MAC DONNELL.

I.

One night, my eyes, in seal'd repose,
  Beheld wild war's terrific vision—
When lo ! beside my couch arose
  The Banshee bright, of form Elysian !
Her dark hair's flow stream'd loose below
  Her waist to kiss her foot of lightness ;
The snows that deck the cygnet's neck,
  Would fail to peer her bosom's whiteness !

II.

I saw her—mild her angel mien ;
  Her azure eye was soul-subduing ;
Her white round breast and lip were seen
  The eye of wonder ever wooing—

principal haunts of the fairy host, is valuable, if it were only for its delineation of the mythological topography of the country.

Ⱥ ḣaol-ċoṗ ⱃeanꝫ, a ṗéiꝫ-ċⱃoḃ leaḃaiⱃ,
Ⱥ caol ⱄⱃoiꝫ ṫeaṅ, aꝺéiꝺ 'ⱃa maⱃlⱫe ;
Iⱃ ꝼioⱃ ꝫuⱃ ḃaoiḃiṅ liṅ a ⱃnuaḋ,
Ḃioċ ꝫuⱃ ṫⱃuaꝫ ṁé aꝫ aⱀ cclearaⱫe.

III.

Ⱥⱀ uaiⱃ ṫeaⱃcaⱃ i ꝺo ḃioꝫaⱃ ⱃuaⱃ,
Ꝫo ḃꝼioⱀaiṅ uaiꝺi ca'ⱃ ba aⱃ í ;
Nioⱃ ꝼⱃioꝺal ⱃí, ꝺo ⱃꝫeiṅ ⱃi uaiⱃ,
'S ḃioⱃ ꝫo ꝺuaiⱀc ꝺéiⱃ ṁo ⱃⱄaⱃaⱫe :
Ꝺ'éiꝫioⱃ ꝫo lóṁ ⱀa ꝺéiꝫ le ꝼoṅ,
Nioⱃ aoⱀⱄa lioṁ 'ⱃ ṁé 4 ⱀeaⱃaⱫe
Ꝫuⱃ leaⱀaⱃ i ꝺoⱀ ⱄiⱃ ba ṫuaiⱃ,
Ꝫo ⱃiⱄ ⱀa ⱀꝪⱃuaꝫaċ cé ꝫuⱃ ḃꝼaꝺa í.

IV.

Ⱅiꝫiṁ aⱀioⱃ aⱃiⱃ ꝺo ⱀuaiꝫ,
Ꝫo ⱃiⱄ Cⱃuaċⱀa, 'ⱃ ꝫo ⱃiⱄ SeaⱀaⱫe ;
Ꝫo ⱃiⱄ aoiḃiṅ, aoiꝫeaⱃꝺa, ⱀuaꝺ,
Ⱳaⱃ a ṁḃiꝺ ⱀa ⱃluaꝫa ⱀe ⱄaoiḃ ⱀa beaṅaⱫe
Ꝫo ḣaolḃⱃoꝫ Bóiṅ Ⱥoⱀꝫaiⱃ Oiꝫ,
Ⱥꝫ ꝼéaċaiⱀ ⱀeóiⱀaṁ, 'ⱃ aꝫ ꝺéaⱀaṁ ꝼeaⱃⱄaⱫe
Ni ⱃaiḃ a ⱄuaiⱃⱃⱫ ⱃioⱃ ⱀá ⱃuaⱃ,
Ⱥċꝺ i ꝺo ꝫluaiⱃeaċꝺ ⱄⱃé ⱀa bealaⱫe.

V.

Ⱅiꝫiṁ ꝫo ⱃiⱄ ⱀⱀc liⱃ ⱀa ccⱃuaċ,
Ꝫo cⱃaoiḃ Ruaḋ, 'ⱃ ⱄiꝫiṁ ꝫo Ⱅeaṁaiⱃ ;
Ꝫo ⱃiⱄ ċⱀoc Fiⱃⱀṅ, aoiḃiṅ, ꝼuaⱃ,
'S Ⱥoiḃill Ruaḋ ⱀe ⱄaoiḃ ⱀa cⱃaⱫe :

Her sylph-like waist—her forehead chaste—
　　Her ivory teeth and taper finger—
'Twas heaven, 'tis true, these charms to view—
　　'Twas pain within their sphere to linger !

III.

" Fair shape of light ! thy lowly slave
　　Entreats thy race—thy travels' story."
Her white arm gave one beck'ning wave—
　　She vanish'd like a beam of glory !
My questioning call unheeded all,
　　My cries above the breezes swelling,
As, fill'd with woe, I northward go,
　　To Grugach's distant, fairy dwelling !

IV.

Through fair Senai—through Crochan's hall
　　I wildly chase the flying maiden ;
By fairy fort—by waterfall,
　　Where weird ones wept, with sorrow laden !
My footsteps roam great Aongus' dome,
　　Above the Boyne, a structure airy—
In hall and moat these wild words float,
　　" She onwards treads the haunt of Faëry !"

V.

Mac Lir, I sought thy proud abode—
　　Through Creeveroe my question sounded—
Through Temor's halls of state I strode,
　　And reach'd Cnoc-Fhirinn spell-surrounded,

E

Bhí céaᵒ bean óᵹ, ba réiⁿe clóᵼ,
    Aᵹ éirᵼeaꝼ ceoil 'ꞅ aᵹ ᵼéanaiⁿ airᵼiᵹe,
A bꝛoċaiꞃ Aoibill 'ꞅ ꞃioᵹnaᵼ ᵼuaᵼṁuiⱨaiⁿ,
    'S ṁile ᵹꞃuaᵹaċ ᵹlé le ᵹairᵹiᵼe!

VI.

Ɗo bí aⁿ ᵼꞃiᵼ-bean, ᵼꞃiᵼleaċ, ᵼꞃuaiꞃc,
    Ɗo ċiⁿꞃ aiꞃ buaiꞃᵼ me aⁿ paᵼaiᵹe;
Na ꞃⁿᵹe ᵹo maoineaċ, miⁿ-ᵹeal, ꞃuaꞃ,
    'S a ᵼlaoi-ċuaċa léi ᵹo ⱨalᵼaiᵹe:
Ɗꝼéaċ a ⁿall ᵹo maoꞃᵼa, ⱨall,
    Ba léiꞃ ᵼi aiꞃ ball ᵹuꞃ ⱨé ᵼo leaⁿ í,
Aiꞃ ꞃí 'ꞅ ᵼꞃuaᵹ líⁿ ᵼo ċuaiꞃᵼ,
    Ꞇiᵹ anuaꞃ 'ꞅ éiꞃᵼ aꞃ cceaꞃnaiᵹe.

VII.

"Aⱨo ċⁿeaᵼ," aiꞃ ꞃí, "mo bꞃⁿoⁿ aiꞃ buaiꞃᵼ,
    Aⱨo ᵼiꞃ, mo ꝼluaᵹ, ⁿo laoċꞃaᵼ ᵹairᵹiᵼe;
Ɗo ċꞃeaċ a cciꞃioċaᵼ Caoⁿiⁿᵼicc, ċꞃuaiᵼ,
    Ɗo lioⁿꞃaᵼ luaiᵼ na ᵼᵼꞃéan ᵼᵼꞃeaꞃaiᵹe:
Aⱨaꞃ bíᵼ ꝼaoi ċeó ᵹan bꞃíᵹ ᵹaċ ló
    Ꝼá ċⁿⁿᵹ an bꞃóⁿ ꝼaoi na ᵹallⁿᵹe;
Iꞅ iomaᵼ mac ᵼiliꞃ ᵼibeaꞃᵼa uaim,
    'S a Ċꞃioꞅᵼ naċ ᵼꞃuaᵹ ⱨé na ⁿeaꞃbaiᵹe!"

VIII.

Ɗ'ꝼiaꝼꞃaiᵹeaꞃ ᵼi cia í an bⱨaᵼⁿ
    Ɗ'aoiꞅ an Ꞇiᵹeaꞃna beaᵼ an ꝼeaꞃ ᵹꞃoiᵼe,
Na Ꞃíᵹ aiꞃ ᵹaoiᵼil ᵹo bꞃioᵹⁿiaꞃ, ᵼiaⁿ,
    Aᵹ ᵼibiꞃᵼ ꝼiaᵼ ꞃⁿc ó na ⱨallⁿᵹe,

By Aoivil-roe, 'mid wine-cups' flow,
    A thousand maids' clear tones were blending ;
And chiefs of the Gael, in armed mail,
    At tilt and tourney were contending !

VI.

The Smooth-skin fair, whose witching eye
    Had lur'd me from my pillow dreamy,
'Mid shadowy hosts was seated high,
    Her coal-black tresses wild and streamy—
She said, while shone her proud glance on
    The form she knew that long pursued her,
" We much deplore thy wanderings sore,
    Now list our wrongs from the fierce intruder."

VII.

" I weep, I weep, my woe-struck bands,
    My country, hosts, and chiefs of bravery—
The cold, rude Alien spoil'd their lands,
    And ground their strength in bitter slavery ;
Crush'd, weak, obscure, they now endure
    Dark sorrow's yoke beneath the stranger ;
And the True and High in exile sigh—
    Heaven, how I need each brave avenger !"

VIII.

" Say, O say, thou being bright !
    When shall the land from slavery waken ?
When shall our hero claim his right,
    And tyrants' halls be terror shaken ?"

Ɗo ɔúṅ ɼj a beól nj ṫuḃaɼꞇ njoɼ mó
Seo 'ɲ ɼjuḃal maɲ ceó j nó maɲ ɼjӡe-ӡaoɼꞇ,
'S njl cúnꞇaɼ ⼝óɼ le ꞇaḃaɼꞇ a ccojɲ
Ca ḣaṁ ɔo ⼝ójnⱄjɔeaɲ ajɼ aɲ ɲeaɼḃajӡe !

——:o:——

ꟾꟾꟾꟾꟾꟾꟾ ӡeal ꞇsuaṁɼujḋ.

I.

Ɯajɔjɲ ӡeal ꞇɼaṁɲajɔ, cojɼ aḃaɲ aɲ Ɍjӡe,[*]
Ⱄeaɲcaɼ aɲ cⱃjlⱄjoṅ ṫⱃéjmɲeaṫ, ɔoṅ ;
Ba ḃjṅe a beul-ӡuꞇ joɲa ɼjaɼáɲ ɼluaӡ ɼjӡe,
Ba ӡjle a ӡɲuaɔ 'ɲá cɼɼe ɲa ꞇꞇoṅ—
Ꙇ cⱃmjɲ caol cajlce—a ꞇɼojӡjɲ caol ꞇeaɲ
Ꙇ ӡaḃájl le ⱄoṅ ⱄaoj ⱄáɼajӡjḃ le ⱄáɲ—
Ꙇɼ mjɼj ӡo mⱃṅꞇe, a ӡjle ó'ɲ ɲӡleaṅ,
Ɯuɲa ꞇꞇjocⱄajɔ ꞇú leaṁ nj ḃéjɔ mjɼj ɼláɲ !

II.

Ꙇṅ uajɼ ɼuӡaɔ aɲ cⱃjlⱄjoṅ ṫájɲjc beaṫ bjṅ,
Le cjoꞇ meala mjɲe ajɼ a caeɲ beol ;
Ṗóӡaɼ-ɼa aɲ cⱃjlⱄjoṅ cúṁɲa, ӡeal, ӡɲjṅ,
Ba ӡɲejɔeaṅaṫ ꞇaɲ ljṅ aꞇꞇ éjɼꞇjӡ le ṁⱃӡeól—
Ċuajɔ ɔealӡ a ӡɲjoɼ ӡⱃb maɲ ċealӡ ꞇɼé m' ċɼojṫe,
Ɗⱄáӡ mé ӡaɲ ḃɼjӡ ӡjɔ bɼóɲaṫ le ɲáɔ,
Naṫ jonӡaɲꞇaṫ beó me le cealӡ ꞇɼé m' ċɼojṫe,
Na céaɔa ɔo claojɔeaṫ ɲóṁaṁɼa ɔá ӡɲáɔ !

---

* *Abhan-an Righe*, a river of the County Kilkenny. It is called *Avonree*, or the *King's River*, from the death of the monarch, Niall, who, about the middle of the ninth century, was drowned in its

She gives no sign—the form divine
  Pass'd like the winds by fairies woken—
The future holds, in Time's dark folds,
  The despot's chain of bondage broken !

———:o:———

ONE CLEAR SUMMER MORNING.

I.

One clear summer morning, near blue Avonree,
  A stately brown maiden flash'd full on my way ;
More white was her brow than the foam of the sea ;
  More holy her voice than the fairy choir's lay !
Her slight waist was chalk-white, her foot light and
    smooth
  Glanc'd air-lifted over the wild, grassy slope—
" Fair light of the valley," I said to her sooth,
  " My heart's health is gone if you yield me no
    hope !"

II.

At the birth of the maiden, a humming bee flew,
  With a rich honey-shower, to her berry-red lip—
I snatch'd, from the fair one, the sweet, fragrant dew ;
  'Twas rapture entrancing—but what did I sip ?
A sting from her red lip sped, swift as a dart,
  Its way to my bosom—how woful to say ;
'Tis strange that I live with the barb in my heart,
  While thousands have died of her love since that
    day !

waters during a flood, while he was endeavouring to preserve the
life of a soldier of his train who had been swept into the current
of the river.

Uaill-ʒuc an Aoiḃnis.

Ulliaṁ Ḋall, no ċán.

I.

Aiṟ ḃṟuaċ na Coille moiṟe,
Fa ċṟuaḋ-ḃṟataiḋ bṟoiṅ,
Ḋo ṟeolaḋ ʒuc aṁ ċluaṟaḋ,
Ba ṟuaiṟce liom, ṟá ḋo,
Na ceol na cṟiʒc iṟ ṟuaiṁiṅ
A'ṟ na ʒloṟ na loṅ ṟa ṅ-uaiʒṅeaṟ
Ḋo be ceol ba ḃiṅṅe aiṟ cuaiṟḋ liom,
Ḋa ʒ-cualaḋ ḋoṅ c-ṟoiṟc.

II.

Ná'ṅ ceol ḋo ċuʒaiḋ ṟuaiʒ fiṟ
Caṟ moṟ ṁiṟ ó'ṅ Ṟoiṁ,
Na aṅ ṟpoiṟc ḋo ḋeiṅiḋ ʒṟuaʒaiḋ
A ʒ-cṟuaiḋ-liṟ na ṟluaʒ
Ná'ṅ ʒeoiṅ ḋo leiʒiḋ cuaċa
ʒo ṅuaḋ ċoiṟ coille a ṁ-ḃṟuaċ cṅoic ;
A'ṟ ʒaċ bṟoṅ ʒuṟ ċṟṟ mo ċuaiṟḋ ḋiom
Ṁuṅa ṁ-beaḋ Ṁallaiʒe beaʒ O !

III.

Saiċe beaċ ḋo luḋaʒ liṅṅ
Aiṟ ċuaiṟiṟʒ a c-ṟṟeoiṅ,*
Aṅ foʒṁaṟ ḋo beaḋ ʒo buaḋaṟta
A'ṟ ʒaṅ ṟualcaiṟ aiʒ Seoṅ

---

* The poet, seeing a swarm of bees confused and wild at the loss

THE VOICE OF JOY.

I.

By Kilmore's woody highland,
  Wandering dark and drear,
A voice of joy came o'er me,
  More holy to mine ear
Than wild harp's breathing dreamy,
  Or blackbird's warbling streamy;
No seraph choir could frame me
  Such soft music dear!

II.

More sweet than anthems holy
  Brought seaward from Rome,
Than spells by wizards spoken
  O'er stolen maiden's doom,
Or cuckoo's song inspiring
  Where woods green hills environ—
Save love for one fair siren,
  It banish'd my gloom.

III.

The golden bees were ranging
  The air for a chief—
'Twas freedom's trumpet woken,
  And dark tyrants' grief;

of the queen bee, accepts the omen as a prognostic of the destruc-
tion of the English power in Ireland.

Seóinre ꞇap leap ꞇá puaꝣaꝺ
J'r ап cóip ꞇo ḃjoc ꝣo buacac
Ꝣап óp ná bajlꞇe ajp buap ꞇójḃ
J'r пj ꞇruaꝣ ljom a m-bpóp !

IV.

ᵿ Spópajll ꞇá m-bejꝺjpp rjpꞇe
Ƒaoj cpuaꝺ-leac a ꝣ-cojṁeaꝺ,
ᵿ'r ап rꝣéal ro clor map cúalaꝺ
Ꝣo ruapṁap ajp reól ;
Le ƒópra a'r neapꞇ mo ꝣuajlle'
ᵿp ƒóꝺ ꝣo ꝣ-cajꞇƒjp ruar ꝺjom
ᵿ'r me ꞇeacꝺ ꞇap m'ajr ꝣo luajmpeac
Ƒaoj ꞇuajpm ап rꝣeojl !

——:o:——

ᵿJᚱ EJᚱE ПJ JПEOSᵿJП CJᵿ ḣJ.*

I.

ᵿ raojp 'r mé ꞇéappaṁ ap peojp,
ᵿjp ап ꞇaoḃ ejle ꝺop ꞇeópa 'pa mbjm ;
Ꝺo ꞇaoḃpajꝣ ап rpéjp-beap am cójp,
Ꝺƒáꝣ ꞇaompac, bpeojꝺꞇe, laꝣ, rjñ :
Ꝺo ꝣéjlljor ꝺá méjñ 'r ꝺá clóꝺ,
Ꝺá beul ꞇapajꝺ, beó-ṁjljr, bjñ ;
'S ꝣup léjm mé ƒá ꝺéjꝣjp ꝺul pa cójp,
'S ajp Ejpe пj 'peórajp cja ḣj !

* The author of this beautiful love song is unknown; but it would seem that he was a native of the County Kerry, as this is

And George, a homeless ranger—
 His tribe, the faithless stranger,
Far banish'd—and their danger,
 My glad heart's relief!

IV.

If o'er me lay at Shronehill
 The hard flag of doom,
And came that sound of sweetness
 To cheer the cold gloom—
Death's darksome bondage broken,
 My deaf, dull ear had woken,
And, at the spell-word spoken,
 I'd burst from the tomb!

——:o:——

FOR IRELAND I'D TELL NOT HER NAME.

I.

One eve, as I happen'd to stray
 By the lands that are bordering on mine,
A maiden came full on my way,
 Who left me in anguish to pine—
The slave of the charms, and the mien,
 And the silver-ton'd voice of the dame,
To meet her I sped o'er the green ;
 Yet for Ireland I'd tell not her name !

the most popular song in that part of Munster. Tradition attributes it to a young man who fell violently in love with the affianced bride of his own brother.

II.

Ⴃá ᴨɣéɪlꝼɪoċ aᴨ ꞃꝑéɪꞃ-ƀeaᴨ ᴅaᴍ' ɡlóꞃ,
   Ⴎꞃɪaᴅ ꝑáɪóᴄe ᴍo ƀeoɪl ᴅo ƀeɪᴄ ꝼɪoꞃ;
Ɡo ᴅeɪᴎɪᴨ ᴅꞃᴄ ᴅo ᴄéaᴨꝼaɪᴎ ᴅo ɡᴨóᴅ,
Ⴃo léꞃ ċꞃꞃ a ccóꞃ 'ꞃ a ccꞃɪċ:
Ⴃo léɪɡꝼɪᴎ ɡo léꞃ ꞃᴄaɪꞃ ᴅaᴍ ꞃᴄóꞃ,
   'S ba ᴍéɪᴎ lɪoᴍ a ꞃóɡaᴅ óᴍ' ċꞃoɪᴅe,
Ⴃo ƀéaᴨꝼaɪᴎ aᴨ ċꞃaoƀ ᴅɪ 'ᴨa ᴅóɪᴅ;
   'S aɪꞃ Éɪꞃe ᴨɪ 'ᴨeóꞃaɪᴎ cɪa hɪ!

III.

'Ⴚá ꞃꝑéɪꞃƀꞃᴨɡɪoll ᴍaoꞃᴅa, ᴍóᴅaᴨɪꞃl, óɡ,
   Ⴎɪꞃ aᴨ ᴄaoƀ eɪle ᴄo'ᴨ ᴄeóꞃa 'ᴨa ᴍbɪᴍ;
'Ⴚá ꝼéɪle 'ɡuꞃ ᴅaoᴨaċᴄ, 'ꞃ ᴍeóꞃ,
   'S ᴅeɪꞃe ᴨó-ᴨɪóꞃ aᴎ ꞃa ᴍᴨaoɪ:
'Ⴚá ꝼolᴄa léɪ aɡ ᴄᴨᴄɪᴨɪ ɡo ꝼeóꞃ,
   Ɡo cocáᴨaċ, óᴨɪbꞃaċ, bᴨóᴢ,
'Ⴚá laꞃa ɪoᴨa leacꞃᴨ ᴍaꞃ ꞃóꞃ;
   'S aɪꞃ Éɪꞃe ᴨɪ 'ᴨeoꞃaɪᴎ cɪa hɪ!

IV.

Ⴎ ꞃáɪꞃ-ꝼɪꞃ bɪ ꝑáɪᴨᴄeaċ lɪoᴍ ꝼéɪᴨ,
   'S ᴍe áɪᴨɪoᴨɪ ᴄá ᴍꝼéɪᴅɪꞃ lɪoᴍ ꞃɡᴨɪoƀ;
Bheɪᴅᴎ ɡꞃáᴅᴍaꞃ le báꞃ-ċᴨɪꞃ ᴨa ccꞃaoƀ
   Ⴃá ƀꞃaɡaɪᴎ áɪᴨɪɡᴄe ó aoɪᴨe cɪa hɪ?
'Ⴚáɪꞃ cáɪᴨᴄe 'ꞃ ᴨɪ cáꞃ oɪᴨɪ é,
   Ɡuꞃ le ᴅáᴨaċᴄ ᴅo ᴄéɪɡɪᴍ leaᴄ ᴅá ꞃᴨɡeaᴨɪ,
Ⴈɪ ꝼuláɪꞃ ɡo ƀꝼᴨɪl cáɪᴍ aɪꞃ a ꞃɡéɪᴍ,
   Ɡo ƀꝼᴨɪl ᴨáɪᴨe oꞃᴄ a léɪɡeaᴅ ᴅᴨᴎ cɪa hɪ!

II.

Would she list to my love-laden voice,
   How sooth were my vows to the fair;
Would she make me for ever her choice,
   Her wealth would increase by my care—
I'd read her our poets' sweet lays,
   Press close to my wild heart the dame,
Devote to her beauty the bays;
   Yet for Ireland I'd tell not her name!

III.

A maiden young, tender, refin'd,
   On the lands that are bordering on mine,
Hath virtues and graces of mind,
   And features surpassingly fine;
Blent amber and yellow compose
   The ringleted hair of the dame,
Her cheek hath the bloom of the rose;
   Yet for Ireland I'd tell not her name!

STANZAS SUPPLEMENTARY TO THE FOREGOING.

IV.

Sweet poet! incline to my prayer—
   For O! could my melodies flow,
I'd sing of your ringleted fair,
   If haply her name I could know.
You are censur'd, permit me to say,
   Nor grieve I you suffer the blame—
Some blot doth her beauty display,
   When for Ireland you'd tell not her name!

v.

21 Bḣṅúṅa15 ! ḟıṅ clúṁa1l ʒaṅ ċaıṁ,
Nıoṅ ḃ-ıoṅʒṅa lıoṁ rⱪáıle ʋaṅ ⱪıṅ ;
Nó ⱪṅ́rʒ ʋo ḃeıⱦ ⱦaḃaⱪⱦa ʋo iṅáıḃ,
Ʒo ṁbeıⱦ ⱳoñ aıⱪ a ʒcáıl ʋo ⱪṅ́ⱦ rıoⱪ ;
Seaċ uʒʋaⱪ ʋo ḟıuḃalaⱶ a láṅ,
O'ṅ Sıⱪ́ⱪ ʒo ⱦⱦı́' aṅ raıle coıⱪ lao1,
Ⱦeaċⱦ ċuʒaṁ-ra aʒ ⱳáʒaıl cúṅⱦaıⱪ aṁ ḃáb,
'S aıⱪ Θıⱪe ṅá ⱦⱪáċⱦⱳⱪ́ⱪ cıa ḣı́ !

——:o:——

BⱤUJNƷJOLL BƵJLC ƵⱦḢ SƵƵⱲNƵJS,*

Ⱳoñ, " Poⱪⱦ Ʒóⱪⱳoṅ."

I.

21 2Uḣáıⱪe a ʒⱪáⱶ ır ⱦu ⱦáṁ' ċⱪáⱶ,
Oċ ! ⱦaḃaıⱪ ʋo láṁ ʒo ʋlⱪ́ⱦ ⱶaṁ?
'S ʒuⱪ ʋual ʋaṁ buaⱶ ṅa cⱪ́ʒe ʋ'ⱳaʒaıl,
Ʒo bⱪáⱦ ṅá ʋéaṅ ṁe ʋıúlⱦaⱶ—
21 cⱪ́l ṅa ṅʋual aⱪé.ṁo ċuṁaⱶ ʒo buaṅ,
Naċ ḃⱳⱪ́lıṁ leaⱦ ⱳuaıⱶⱦe a ccleaṁⱪaⱪ,
Béıⱶeaʋ ʒo ʋuaıⱪc ⱳá ⱪıoⱪ ʒⱪuaıṁ,
2Uⱶá bıⱶıⱪ a ḃⱳaⱶ uaıⱪⱪe a aⱳṅⱪaċⱦ !

* *Baile-ath-Shamhnais.* Ballyhaunis, a market town in the
barony of Costello, County Mayo. It had a monastery for friars of
the order of St. Augustine, endowed by the family of Nangle, who,
in after time, took the name of Costello. It subsisted till the reign
of James I., and at the insurrection of 1641 was restored by some
friars of the same order.—*Lewis's Topographical Dictionary.*

Mr. Hardiman, who leaves this song untranslated in the first
volume of the " Minstrelsy," says that it was composed by a friar

V.

O, Browne, of the pure spotless fame !
  I never would marvel to see
A clown thus consigning to blame
  Those charms that so beautiful be—
But you that have roam'd by the Lee,
  And the scenes of the Suir did proclaim,
Why ask you my secret from me,
  When for Ireland I'd tell not her name ?

——:o:——

THE MAID OF BALLYHAUNIS.

I.

My Mary dear ! for thee I die,
  O ! place thy hand in mine love—
My fathers here were chieftains high,
  Then to my plaints incline, love.
O, Plaited-hair ! that now we were
  In wedlock's band united,
For, maiden mine, in grief I'll pine,
  Until our vows are plighted !

of the monastery of Ballyhaunis, who fell in love with a beautiful
girl of that place. With every respect for the superior informa-
tion of Mr. Hardiman, I beg to say that this lyric, so creditable to
the poetic genius of Connaught, and which stands forth among the
happiest efforts of the pastoral muse of Ireland, was, in all likeli-
hood, written by a youthful student of the monastery, as the second
stanza bears clear proof that the lover is one not arrived at manhood, and who is subject to his father's control.

II.

A bláiṫ na ccaoṁ o ṫápla mé,
  Claoiṫe, ṫréiṫ, le ᵹneaṅn oiᵹṫ;
Tair ꝼaoi m' ḋéiᵹin a ṗíṅ mo ċléiḃ
  'S ᴣabair ᵹráḋ ᵹan ċlaon, ᵹan ċaṁ ᴅaṁ.
Ꝼanaoir ᵹéar! ir me an ceaṅn ᵹan ċéill
  'S ᴅo ċóṁairle m'aṫar ṅíon úṁlᵹear
'S ᵹur b'é cóṁráḋ ᴅéaṅaċ a ᴅúbairᴢ ré liom
  " Tréiᵹre Beul áᴢ ḣaṁnair !

III.

Aċᴅ ᴢuᵹ mé ᵹráḋ ᴅoᴅ ċṅlín bán,
  Air cúl an ᵹáiṅᴅíṅ pónaire;
Doᴅ béiliṅ ᴢláiᴢ mar ċúbar na ᴢráᵹa,
  Doᴅ ᴅá ᵹṅuaḋ ḋearᵹ mar ċaorċon:
Doᴅ beul ir biṅne 'nán ċuaċ air bile,
  'S na ceileabar caoin na ṅeuṅlaiᴢ,
Mo leuṅ 'r mo ṁilleaḋ! ᵹan mé 'r ᴢu a ċumaiṅn,
  Aᵹ éalóᵹaḋ le ṅa ċéile.

IV.

A ᵹráḋ 'r a ṗíṅ ᴅá ṅᵹluairꝼeaḋ liom
  Ᵹo ᴢír na lonᵹ ar Eiṅiṅn ?
Ṅíl ᴢiṅnear ciṅn ná ᴢiṅre cṅoiᴅe,
  Naċ leiᵹċearꝼṅᵹe aṅn ᵹan aṁṗur,
'S ᴢú an ṅeulᴢ eólᴢir ᴢar ṁṅáiḃ na ꝼóᴅla,
  Aᵹur coiṅṅiḋ aᵹaᴅ ꝼéin ó'n mbár me
Oir ᵹan ᵹṅára ᴅé ṅí ṁairꝼiḋ mé,
  Air an ᴢṙáiᴅ ro Bheul áᴢ haṁnair !

II.

Thou, Rowan-bloom, since thus I rove,
    All worn and faint to greet thee,
Come to these arms, my constant love,
    With love as true to meet me!
Alas! my head—its wits are fled,
    I've fail'd in filial duty—
My sire did say, " Shun, shun, for aye
    That Ballyhaunis beauty!"

III.

But thy *Cúilin bán** I mark'd one day,
    Where the blooms of the bean-field cluster,
Thy bosom white like ocean's spray,
    Thy cheek like rowan-fruit's lustre,
Thy tones that shame the wild bird's fame
    Which sing in the summer weather—
And O! I sigh that thou, love, and I
    Steal not from this world together!

IV.

If with thy lover thou depart
    To the Land of Ships, my fair love,
No weary pain of head or heart
    Shall haunt our slumbers there, love—
O! haste away, ere cold death's prey,
    My soul from thee withdrawn is;
And my hope's reward, the churchyard sward,
    In the town of Ballyhaunis!

* *Cúilin bán*, fair flowing hair.

ⱭN Ɑ]NⒹ]R ⱭⱢⱵ]N.

Ⱝn Ⱳⱥnzⱥⱁⱃe Súzⱥɕ, ⱃó cán.

I.

J꜀ ⱃⱀéⱁⱅ ⱅe ꜀eⱥꝇ '꜀ⱥ꜀ ⱏⱥnn,
Ⱳo ꜁né ⱄo ⱋeⱥⱅ ⱄo ꝇon,—
Ⱄ'eⱥꝇⱥ꜁꜁ cneⱥⱄ—
J꜀ ꜀ⱥ꜁zeⱥⱄ '꜀ ⱄeⱥ꜀ⱅ
Ⱝⱁ ⱥoⱅ, ⱥⱁ ꜀꜁ⱥ꜀ⱅ, ⱥⱁ ɕoⱁ.
Ⱄo ⱅ꜀éⱁ꜁ ⱁe ⱁ꜀ ꝏⱥ꜀ ⱁo ꜁꜀eⱥnn,
'Ⱅá'n ɕꝏéⱃ꜀ ⱥ neⱥ꜀꜀ⱥⱁⱄ ꝇⱁoⱁ ;—
J꜀ ⱅⱥoⱅ ⱁo ⱅeⱥ꜀ⱅ,
J꜀ ꝏⱥon ⱁo neⱥ꜀ⱅ,—
Ⱄo ɕꝏⱥoⱁ—ⱄo ꜀zⱥⱁ꜀ ⱁo ⱁeⱥⱅⱥⱃ꜀ !

II.

Ⱡe ⱨé꜁zⱃon zeⱥⱁ ⱄoⱁ ꜀ⱐoⱄⱥ꜀ⱐꝅꝇ,
Ⱝ ꜀ⱃ ꜀é꜃꜀ⱃon ⱄeⱥ꜀ ⱥⱁ Ⱨⱨ꜀ó꜁ⱥ ;*
Ⱄo ꜀ⱐéⱥⱄⱥⱃ꜁ ⱥ꜀ⱁꝅꝇⱅ
Ⱄⱥo꜀ ⱥⱁ ⱥⱃce—
Ⱝ ꜀é ⱅeⱃ꜀ ꜀eⱥ꜀z ⱁo ꜀ⱥⱐⱃꝅꝇ.
'Ⱅá ⱥ c꜀ⱥoⱅꝏoꝇⱅ ⱅⱥⱃ꜀ zo ⱅonn,
ꜱo nⱃⱥ꜀ⱐⱄⱥɕ, c꜀ⱥⱅⱥɕ, c꜀oⱁ :
J꜀ ⱥ ꜀ⱃn-꜀o꜀z ꜀eⱥ꜀
Ⱡe zⱥeⱅ꜃ⱅ ⱥ ꜀ꝇⱥⱄ
Nⱥ céⱥⱄⱅⱥ ꝏeⱥ꜀ zo ꝏⱥnn.

---

* *Brogha*, Bruff, a town in the County of Limerick.

THE LOVELY MAID.

I.

Long, long I'm worn and weak,
And pale my wasted cheek;
    And groans have rent
    Where shafts were sent
My inmost soul to seek—
My sense of joy is dead,
The Church's wrath I dread;
    I'm wild, unwise,
    My vigour dies,
My wits are scattered, fled!

II.

The love I do avow
The beauteous Star of Brogha,
    Hath heap'd dark blame
    Upon my name,
And withering left me now—
Her hair, in wreathed flow,
Falls shining, quivering, low;
    Her rich, ripe eye
    Bids thousands die
Beneath its arrowy glow!

III.

Τá a beul bịnn blarτa, buaòaċ,
'S a ὁέịὁ ịḣịon ċaịlce ċúṁanɜ,
    Ἀ ṗéịὁ-ċnoḃ ὁeaṛ,
    Ἀ h-aol-ċoṛp ṛeanɜ,
Ἀ ṛɜéịṁ ṁaṛ alaò aịṛ ṛṇụ́ll.
Ἀ ccéịn a τeaċτ ɜo ṛụ́ɜaċ,
'S na τéτe a ḟṇeaṛὁal ὁṇ́ịṇṇ;
    Φo ċéaṛnaịὁ ịṛ ḟeaṛ
    Ἀṇ ḃéịτ le m' aịṛ,
Φo ċlaoṇ, ὁo ṛɜaṛ mo lúτ.

IV.

Φo ḟléaċὁaṛ ṛeal ὁaṁ' ṇ́uṇ,
Le h-éịɜịon ɜean ὁá ɜṇ́ṛ;
    Φo ḃéịc, ὁo ṛɜṇeaὁ,
    Φo léịm ὁo ṗṇeaḃ,
"Seṇn me ḟeaṛὁa"—aὁúḃaịṛτ—
Ṅị ċaịllḟịoὁ ḟéịn mo ċlú
Le ṗéịc ɜan ṇaịτ, ṁaṛ τú,
    Le ḃṛéaɜ ịṛ beanτ
    Φo leṇn—ὁo ḟlaὁ
Na céaὁτa bean ṛa Ṁuṁaịn!

——:o:——

CUịSle ᴍo ĊROịῆe.

I.

Ἀịṛ maịὁịn a nae ṛoịṁ ɜṇéịn ɜo moċ,
    Φo ὁéaṛcaṛ an ḃéịτ ba ṁaịṁὁa cṛuτ;

III.

Lips, precious, musical,
Teeth, chalk-white, close-set, small;
  Hand, smooth, and fair;
  Form, statelier
Than wave-pois'd swan withal—
Once favouring heaven did will
That, downward o'er the hill,
  Beside me came
  The light-limb'd dame—
Faint tremblings through me thrill!

IV.

Low kneeling to the fay,
I vainly made essay
  To melt her heart—
  With shriek and start,
She wildly turn'd away:
" Begone !" the virgin said,
" Seducer, thou'st betrayed,
  " With deed of guile,
  " And tale and wile,
" Full many a Munster maid !"

——:o:——

PULSE OF MY HEART.

I.

Before the sun rose at yester-dawn,
I met a fair maid adown the lawn:

Sneaċꞇa aᵹuꞱ caon ḃí aᵹ caiꞃminꞇ, 'na Ʇᵹéiṁ
'S a ꞃeanᵹa-ċoꞃp ꞃéiṁ maꞃ ᵹéiꞱ aiꞃ Ʇꞃuꞇ;
'S a ċꞃꞃle mo ċꞃoiꞋe! cꞃéaꞋ í 'n ᵹꞃuaiꞂꞀ
ꞱiꞀ oꞃꞇ?

II.

BuꞋ ḃinne ᵹuꞇ caoiꞀ a béil le Ʇulꞇ
Ná OꞃꞂeuꞃ Ꞌo léiᵹ ᵹo ꞂaoꞀ na ꞇoiꞃc;—
Ḃꞌí a ꞃaṁaꞃ-Ꞁoꞃᵹ ꞀéiꞋ maꞃ ċꞃioꞱꞇal na mḃꞃaoꞀ
Aiꞃ ꞃeamaiꞃ-ᵹlaiꞱ ꞃéiꞃ Ꞁoiṁ ᵹꞃéiꞀ ᵹo moċ;
'S a ċꞃꞃle mo ċꞃoiꞋe! cꞃéaꞋ í an ᵹꞃuaiꞂꞀ
ꞱiꞀ oꞃꞇ?

——:o:——

A ꞆAIA SIꞀꞆE AIꞂ ꞆO ꞆꞃUAAꞂA.

I.

AꞇáiꞂ Ʇinꞇe aiꞃ Ꞌo ꞇuamba,
A'Ʇ ꞇo ᵹeabaiꞃ anꞀ Ꞌo ꞃioꞃ mé;
Ꞇá mḃéiꞋeaꞋ báꞀ Ꞌo Ꞌá láṁ 'ᵹam,
Ní ꞱᵹaꞀꞂainꞀ leaꞇ ċoiꞋċe—
A úbailíꞀ aᵹuꞱ anꞀꞱacꞇ,
IꞱ am ꞋaiꞀꞃa liᵹe leaꞇ,
'Ꞇá bolaꞋ Ꞃuaꞃ na cꞃiaꞋ oꞃꞀi,
Ꞌaꞇ na ᵹꞃéiꞀe 'Ʇ na ᵹaoiꞇe!

II.

Aꞇá cló aiꞃ mo ċꞃoiꞋeꞃ,
'Ꞇá lioꞀꞇa le ᵹꞃáꞋ Ꞌꞃꞇ,
LionꞀꞋuḃ aiꞃ ꞇaoḃ ꞃioꞱ Ꞌe,
Cóṁ ciaꞃ Ꞌuḃ le h-áiꞀꞀe.

The berry and snow
To her cheek gave its glow,
And her bosom was fair as the sailing swan—
Then, pulse of my heart! what gloom is thine?

II.

Her beautiful voice more hearts hath won
Than Orpheus' lyre of old had done ;
    Her ripe eyes of blue
    Were crystals of dew,
On the grass of the lawn before the sun—
And, pulse of my heart! what gloom is thine?

——:o:——

FROM THE COLD SOD THAT'S O'ER YOU.

I.

From the cold sod that's o'er you
    I never shall sever—
Were my hands twin'd in your's, love,
    I'd hold them for ever—
My fondest, my fairest,
    We may now sleep together,
I've the cold earth's damp odour,
    And I'm worn from the weather!

II.

This heart, fill'd with fondness,
    Is wounded and weary ;
A dark gulf beneath it
    Yawns jet-black and dreary—

2ᴌá baꞁꞁꞁoꞁ aoꞁ ꞁꞁꞁꞇ ꝺaꞁꞁ,
'S ꝺo cclaoꞁꝺꝼeaꝺ aꞁ báꞁ ꞁꞁe,
Béꞁꝺeaꝺꞁa ꞁꞁ' ꞁꞁoꞇ-ꝛaoꞁꞇe,
Kóꞁꞁaꝺ ꞁꞁoꞁ aꞁꞁ ꞁa báꞁꞇa !

III.

Nuaꞁꞁ ꞁꞁ ꝺóꞁꝛ le ꞁꞁo ꞁꞁꞁꞁꞁꞇꞁꞁ,
ꝛo ꞁꞁbꞁꞁꞁꞁe aꞁꞁ ꞁꞁo leaba ;
2ꞁꞁ ꝺo ꞇuaꞁꞁba ꞁeaꝺ bꞁꝺꞁꞁꞁ ꞁꞁꞁꞇe
O oꞁꝺꞇe ꝛo ꞁꞁaꞁꝺꞁoꞁ ;
2ꝛ cuꞁꞁ ꞁꞁoꞁ ꞁꞁo ꞁꞁꞁuaꝺꞇaꞁꞁ,
'S aꝛ cꞁꞁuaꝺ-ꝛol ꝛo ꝺaꞁꞁꝛꞁoꞁꞁ,
Cꞁꞁe ꞁꞁo ꞁaꞁlꞁꞁ cꞁꞁꞁꞁ, ꞁꞇuꞁꞁaꝺ,
ꝺo luaꞇaꝺ ꞁꞁoꞁꞁ ꞁa leaꞁꞇ !

IV.

2ꞁꞁ cꞁꞁꞁꞁꞁ leaꞇꞁa aꞁꞁ oꞁꝺꞇe,
ꝺo bꞁoꞁa 'ꝛuꞁ ꞇuꞁa ;
Fá buꞁꞁ aꞁꞁ cꞁꞁaꞁꞁꞁ ꝺꞁꞁaꞁꝛꞁꞁꝛ,
'S aꞁꞁ oꞁꝺꞇe aꝛ cuꞁꞁ cꞁꞁꞁꞁꞁe ;
Céaꝺ ꞁꞁolaꝺ le ꞁ-ꞁoꞁa,
Naꞁꞁ ꝺeáꞁꞁaꞁꞁaꞁꞁ aꞁꞁ ꞁꞁꞁlleaꝺ,
'S ꝛo bꞁꞁꞁl ꝺo ꞁꞁoꞁꞁóꞁꞁ ꞁꞁaꞁꝛꝺeaꞁꞁꞁꞁ,
Na cꞁaꞁꞁꞁ ꞁoꞁllꞁe aꞁ ꝺo ꞁꞁoꞁꞁꞁꞁe !

V.

Cá ꞁa Saꝛaꞁꞁꞇ 'ꞁ ꞁa Bꞁáꞁꞇꞁe,
ꝛaꞁꞁ lá ꞁꞁoꞁꞁ a bꞁeaꞁꝛ ;
ꝺo ꞁꞁoꞁꞁ beꞁꞇ a ꞁꝛꞁáꝺ leaꞇ,
2 óꞁꝛbeaꞁ ꞁꞁ ꞇú ꞁꞁaꞁꞁb ;

When death comes, a victor,
   In mercy to greet me,
On the wings of the whirlwind,
   In the wild wastes you'll meet me !

III.

When the folk of my household
   Suppose I am sleeping,
On your cold grave, till morning,
   The lone watch I'm keeping ;
My grief to the night wind,
   For the mild maid to render,
Who was my betrothed
   Since infancy tender !

IV.

Remember the lone night
   I last spent with you, love,
Beneath the dark sloe-tree,
   When the icy wind blew, love—
High praise to the Saviour
   No sin-stain had found you,
That your virginal glory
   Shines brightly around you !

V.

The priests and the friars
   Are ceaselessly chiding,
That I love a young maiden,
   In life not abiding—

Ḃéanḟaiṁ foṛзaḋ aiṛ an nзaoiṫ ḋṛṫ
'S ḋion ḋṛṫ ó'n ḃfeaṛṫaiṁ :
Aзuṛ cṁaḋ ҙéan ṁo cṅoiḋeṛi
Ċiṛ ḃeiṫ ṛioṛ aṁṛa ṫṫalaṁ !

VI.

Ċaḃaiṛ ḋo ṁallaċṫ ḋoḋ ṁáṫaiṛín,
'S áiṛṁiṛḋṛi ṫ-aṫaiṛ ;
'S a ṁaiṛṛion ḋoḋ cáiṛḋe,
Зo léiṛeaċ na ṛeaṛaṁ :
Náṛ léiз ḋaṁ ṫṛ ṗóṛaḋ
'S ṫu heó 'зaṁ aḋ ḃeaṫa,
Aзuṛ naċ n-iaṛṛḟaiṛn maṛ ṛṛṛéiḋ leaṫ,
Aċ líҙḋe lioṁ aiṛ leaba !

——:0:——

Be 'N EIRINN I ṀO ҙRAḊ I.

An Ṁanзaiṛe Sṛзaċ, ṛó cáṛ.

I.

Cé faḋa ṁé le h-aeṛ an ṫ-ṛaoҙail,
Iṛ зuṛ loiṫeaṛ béiṫ a'ṛ céaḋ ṁá'ṛ ḟioṛ,
Nioṛ ḋeaṛcaṛ aon ḋo léiṛ зoiṛ ṛínn,
Зo ṫeaċṫ aṁ ṛliҙe ḋo 'n báṛ-cṅeiṛ—
Sí an cṛíḟionn caoiṛ-ṫaiṛ зṛáḋṁaṛ,
Lé зaeṫe ṁiṛll ṁo ṛláiṛṫe,
Aon зaṛ ṗuiṛṛ,
Зaṛ ṫaoṁ, зaṛ ṫeiṁioll,
Bé 'n Eiṛiṛn í, ṁo ҙṛáḋ í !

O ! I'd shelter and shield you,
 If wild storms were swelling,
And O ! my wreck'd hope,
 That the cold earth's your dwelling!

VI.

Alas, for your father,
 And also your mother,
And all your relations,
 Your sister and brother,
Who gave you to sorrow,
 And the grave 'neath the willow,
While I crav'd, as your portion,
 But to share your chaste pillow !

——:o:——

WHOE'ER SHE BE, I LOVE HER.

I.

Through pleasure's bowers I wildly flew,
Deceiving maids, if tales be true,
Till love's lorn anguish made me rue
 That one young Fair-neck saw me,
 Whose modest mien did awe me,
 Who left my life to hover
  O'er death's dark shade—
  The stainless maid,
Whoe'er she be, I love her !

II.

Ir cpaṫaċ, cpaoḃaċ, péjṫ a ꭤlaojṡ,
Njl ceal 'na rṡéjṁ, nj 'l claon 'na cpojṫe ;
Ꮯa majre a'r méjn ꭤa ṁéjꭤ 'ra mnaoj,
Ṡan ṡaoṫ le rṅṡeaṅj 'na cájl ṡlan ;
'Sj an ḃéjṫ ꭤo claojꭤjṡ na ᴄájnᴄe,
le ɦ-éjṡjon ṡpjnn ꭤa bán-ċnejr,
Ꮃajʈ aon ċṅʈ rj
Ꭿ n-eaṡ ċpṅṫ rjnn,
Ḃé 'n Cjpjnn j, mo ṡpáꭤ j !

III.

Ir ꭤear a ꭤéjꭤ, a beul, 'ra pjob,
Ꭿ mala ċaol, 'ra claon-porṡ pjṡjn,
Jona leacajn ꝥejc an ċaoʈ 'ra ljꭤ,
Ꮃajʈ ṡéjr ajʈ ljnn, a bán cpuṫ ;
Ꮯa ꝥéjle, a'r ꝥjnne, 'r ꝥájlᴄe
'Ṡ an m-ḃéjṫ 'naʈ ṫujl a cájne,
Nj baoṫ a ṡnjojṅj,
Nj ꭤaoʈ a ꭤljṡe,
Ḃé 'n Cjpjnn j, mo ṡpáꭤ j !

IV.

O ṡaḃara léj maʈ céjle ꝥjoʈ,
Nj rṡaʈꝥaꭤ léj ṡo ꭤ-ᴄejṡeaꭤ ꭤo 'n ċjll,
Ꭿn balram béul-ᴄajr, beuraċ, bjnn,
Do ṡeuʈ-ṡojʈ rjnn le ṡpáꭤ ꭤj—
Ꭿ ṡcéjn ṡan ṁojll ó'r ájll leaᴄ,

II.

Her hair like quivering foliage flows,
Her heart no thought of evil knows,
Her face with purest virtue glows,
    Her fame all hate defying—
    While for her crowds are dying,
    And round death's threshold hover,
        Where I, for one,
        Am nearly gone—
    Whoe'er she be, I love her!

III.

What beauteous teeth, and lip, and neck,
And eye and brow the maiden deck;
What red and white her cheek bespeck!
    Like wave-pois'd swan she's fairest,
    In virtue high she's rarest;
    In her may none discover
        One deed to blame—
        Mild, modest dame,
    Whoe'er she be, I love her!

IV.

But since soft ties are round us wove,
Which nought but death can e'er remove,
That balsam-bearing Lip of love   .
    That spell-bound left me dying—
    Now far together flying

Le céjle paʒaṁ, a ʒráṫ ʒjl,
    An raoʒal nj b-ᵽajʒjʒ
    ʒo h-eaʒ aṗ n-ᴅéjʒlᴄ—
Bé 'n Ejṗjnn j, mo ʒráṫ j!

v.

Raċᵽaᴅ léj ʒo h-Ejṗṗe rjor,
A mearʒ na m-béjᴄ ʒeal aoṗac ʒljṅṅ,
A'r na reabac réjṁe, rearᴅaċ, ʒṗjṅṅ,
    Chuṁ ᵽéjr, a'r ᵽjoṅ, a'r ájleaċᴄ ;
Le h-aoṅᴄa ʒaoṫjl a'r cájṗᴅe,
Béaṗᵽaᴅ j ᴄaṗ rájle,
    An bejᴄ ʒan baojr,
    Jr réjṁe rljʒ,
Bé 'n Ejṗjnn j, mo ʒráṫ j!

vi.

A h-ajṅjṁ raoṗ nj ᴅéaṗᴄaṗ ljṅṅ
A'r ᴅo'ṅ ᴄ-raoʒal cé ṗo ṗjṅjṁ
Jr j ʒan bṗúʒ, ċṗṗ raoʒaᴅ am ċṗojᴅe
    ᴅo léjṗjʒ ᴄjṅṅ ċuṁ bájr mé ;
An ċṗjlᵽjoṅn ṁjn-ᴄear, ṁṅáṁṗjl
Le ʒaeᴄ ᴅo ṁjll mo ᵽlájṅᴄe
    Béjᴄ ʒan ṗṗṁp
    ʒan ᴄaoṁ, ʒan ᴄejṁjol ;
Bé 'n Ejṗjnn j, mo ʒráṫ j!

The ocean-billows over,
    Who can divide
    From me my bride?
Whoe'er she be, I love her!

v.

But first to Eirne's lovely lake,
Where maids are gay, our course we'll take,
Where generous chiefs bright banquets make,
    And purple wine is flowing;
    Then from our dear friends going,
    We'll sail the ocean over,
      I and my dame
      Of stainless fame—
Whoe'er she be, I love her!

vi.

Her secret name I'll not impart,
Although she pierc'd my wandering heart,
With such a death-dispensing dart
    As love-sick left me lying,
    In fiery torment dying,
    Till pity mild did move her—
      But wine of Spain
      To her we'll drain,
Whoe'er she be, I love her

Ban-Ċnuic Aoiḃin Eirionn.

Donnċaḋ Ruaḋ Mac Conmara, cct.

I.

Beir beanaċt ó'm ċroiḋe go tír na h-Eirionn,
   Bán-ċnuic aoiḃin Eirionn,
Cum a mairion do ḟiolraċ Ir a'r Eiḃir*
   A m-bán-cnuic aoiḃin Eirionn—
An áit ion ar b'aoiḃinn binn ġut éan,
Mar ṫáim ċirt caoin ag cruine Gaoḋal;
Sé mo ċár a beiṫ mile mile a gcéin
   O bán-ċnuic aoiḃin Eirionn!

II.

Bion banna boġ rlim air caoin-ċnuic Eirionn,
   Bán-ċnuic aoiḃin Eirionn,
'Sir fearr iona'n tír reo oiṫ gaċ rléiḃe ann,
   Bán-ċnuic aoiḃin Eirionn,
Ba binne na méaraiḃ air téaḋaiḃ ceóil,
Sinim agur ġeimreaċ a laoġ 'r a m-bó,
Agur taitniom na gnéine orṫa aorḋa a'r óg
   Air bán-ċnuic aoiḃin Eirionn!

III.

Aṫáiḋ garna lionṫar a ḋ-tír na h-Eirionn,
   Bán-ċnuic aoiḃin Eirionn,

* Eibher or Eivir, the son of Ir, who, with his brothers, the sons

FAIR HILL'D, PLEASANT IRELAND.

I.

Take a blessing from the heart of a lonely griever,
    To fair-hill'd, pleasant Ireland,
To the glorious seed of Ir and Eivir,
    In fair-hill'd, pleasant Ireland,
Where the voice of birds fills the wooded vale,
Like the mourning harp o'er the fallen Gael—
And oh! that I pine, many long days' sail,
    From fair-hill'd, pleasant Ireland!

II.

On the gentle heights are soft sweet fountains,
    In fair-hill'd, pleasant Ireland;
I would choose o'er this land the bleakest mountains
    In fair-hill'd, pleasant Ireland—
More sweet than fingers o'er strings of song,
The lowing of cattle the vales among,
And the sun smiling down upon old and young,
    In fair-hill'd, pleasant Ireland!

III.

There are numerous hosts at the trumpet's warning,
    In fair-hill'd, pleasant Ireland;

of Milesius, shared Ireland between them. Ir and his son Eivir
had Ulster for their share.

Ⴀ'ᴦ ᵽеапас́оꙇп ᵹпоꙇᴏе па сlаоꙇᴏᵽеас́ с́еаᴏса,
Ⴀꙇп báп-с́пꙉс аоꙇbꙇп Єꙇпꙇопп—
Ⴏⴰ ᴄꙉпᴦе споꙇᴏе а'ᴦ mо с́пꙉппеаᴏ ᴦᵹéаl,
Jаᴏ аᵹ ᵹаllа-ᴕꙉс ᴦꙇоᴦ ᵽа ᵹпеꙇm, mо lеип !
Ⴀ'ᴦ а m-bаꙇlсе ᴏа поꙇпп ᵽа с́ꙇоᴦ ᵹо ᴏаоп,
Ⴀ m báп-с́пꙉс аоꙇbꙇп Єꙇпꙇопп !

——:o:——

CⴀꙆᴄᴙꙆN NꙆ SꙁеOꙆN.*

I.

Sé ап ᵽꙇаᴏаꙇс́е ᴦᴏ Bеапа† ап ᵽеап ᵽꙇаl bꙇ аᵹ
        Bеаllаꙇᵹ
Ⴀᴦ пꙇ'п b'ꙇаᴏса é ᵽá 'п сеас́ᴦо lе lꙉᴏе апп
        аm пóꙇп,
Sа mаꙇᵹᴏеап bᴦеáᵹ bаппаm̓аꙇl пá'п с́ꙉп ᴦpéꙇᴦ
пꙇаm̓ а b-ᵽеапаꙇb,
С́ᴦm ᵹlеᵹс́аl mап ᴦпеас́са ᴦꙇ Сáꙇсᴘꙇп пꙇ Sꙁеóꙇп !

II.

Ⴄá па сеиᴏса ᴏ'á mаса꙲ꙇᴏе ᴏul ап éиᵹспис́ ᴏ'á
        ᴦеапсᴦап,
Rоᴦс пéꙇᴏ ᵹlап с́luаꙇп mеаllа, bеиl сапа mап
        пóᴦ,

---

* This song is the production of a Connaught bard. It seems to be an extempore effusion in praise of the daughter of a western chief, at whose residence the person whom the minstrel styles the *Hunter of Bera*, had arrived. This spirited outburst of song was certainly a characteristic mode of introducing the " Hunter of

And warriors bold, all danger scorning,
    In fair-hill'd pleasant Ireland—
Oh, memory sad ! oh, tale of grief !
They are crush'd by the stranger past all relief ;
Nor tower nor town hath its native chief,
    In fair-hill'd, pleasant Ireland !

——:o:——

CAITRIN, THE DAUGHTER OF JOHN.

I.

Sing the Hunter of Bera, who from Ballagh came
    hither,
    Our gates open'd wide to his coming at noon,
And the virgin whose coldness did suitors' hopes
    wither,
    The snow-waisted Caitrin, the daughter of John !

II.

There are tall sons of bravery that .pine in her
    slavery ;
    Her eye all beguiling—small lips like the rose ;

Bera " to the " Bright Swan of Lough Glynn."
  + *Bera. Bearhaven*, a territory in the south-west of the County
Cork, the patrimony of the O'Sullivan Bear. *Ballagh*, or *Balla*, a
village in the Barony of Claremorris, County Mayo. It has an
ancient round tower.

F

Canbrncaıl a m-bıꝺ bnearˉ ann, bıꝺ ıolnaꝺ ꝣaċ
  ꝺaċa ann,
Ꝣaċ céıb bꞃꝺe léı aꝣ carˉaꝺ ꝣo alꞇaıb 'na ꝺeóıꝣ.

III.

Cá an b'ıonꝣnaꝺ ꝺo'n nezıꞃn aꝣ ꝣaınˉeaꝺ ꝼá Venus,
  Ꝃꝺan ꝺo bı Conċuban ꝼa Ꝺhéꝺnꝺne ꝺul a
  b-pıanꞇaıb ꝺ'á ꝣnáꝺ ;
U néulꞇ eólnꞃ na h-éıꝣꞃ aın cónuꝣaꝺ na ꝣnéꝺne,
  'Sı ꝺo noꝣa ċan mnáıb éıneann ı a ꝺéın a'ꞃa
  ꝣ-cáıl!

IV.

Ꝺeaꝺ-ċunnaꝺ aın ꝺnáıb a cꝺeaꝺ ı, 'ꞃ ı ꝼıalꝺaıꞇ
  an oınıċ ı,
Ꝣaċ reꝺꝺ ꝺearˉ ꝺ'á bnonnaꝺ 'ꞃ ꝺ'á rcaıneaꝺ aın
  luċꞇ ceoıl ;
'Sı ꝺꞃnnın ċlanna Uꝺnꝺneaꝺ ı, 'ꞃı no ꝣnáꝺ na
  b-ꝼıle ı,
éala ꝣleꝣeal loċa Ꝣlınne ı, 'ꞃı Cáıꞇnın nı Sheóın !

——:o:——

ꝺUUN NU SUOıꞃSe.

Un Ꝃꝺanꝣaıne Sꞃꝣaċ, no ċán.

I.

Jr ꝼaꝺa ꝺé a ꝣ-cuꝺaıꝺ ꝣan ꞇꞃꞃꞇ le ꞇeunˉma,
  Ꝣo ꝺub-ċnoıꝺeaċ ꞇnéıꞇ-laꝣ ꞇláıꞇ ꝣan ꞇneoın ;
U'm barcaꝺ aꝣ bꞃn 'ꞃ a'm bnuꝣaꝺ aꝣ baoꞇlaıċ,
  U lꞃb lom rléıbe ꝼaoı bnácaꝺ an bnóın ;

She's a jewel all splendid, of brightest hues blended,
　Each gold-wreathed ringlet to her white ankle
　　flows!

III.

Now why should we wonder if thousands surrender,
　Like Connor to Deirdre, their hearts to her chain ;
Guiding light of the poet, of sun-glancing splendour,
　The fairest in Erin of beauty's bright train !

IV.

O'er her kindred and nation she holds highest station,
　Dispensing rich guerdons to minstrels of song ;
Clan-Murray's fair darling—my harp's inspiration,
　Bright swan of Lough Glynn, beauteous daughter
　　of John !

——:o:——

THE SONG OF FREEDOM.

I.

All woeful, long I wept despairing,
　Dark-bosom'd, fainting, wearied, weak,
The foeman's withering bondage wearing,
　Remote in the gorge of the mountain bleak ;

ʒaη ċαηαιⱄ α'ⱂ ċαⱪαιⱃ αċⱅ ⴹoηη*.'ⱃα ȝαoιⱅα,
'ⴹo ⱪeαⱃⱅⱃȝ αιⱃ ⱄ-ⱅⱃⱃ ⱄαⱂ ⱅⱃⱂⱡιⱗȝ ⱅαeⱪ leιⱃ,
ʒo η-αιⱅⱂιⱃeαⱄ ⱄⱃⱃ ȝαċ ⱂⱃⱗ ⱪⱃⱄ lⱗⱃⱂ ⱄⱃ,
le ⱄⱃⱡ ȝⱂeιⱗⱗ ⱃȝlⱗⱃⱂe α'ⱃ ȝαιⱂⱄeαⱃ ceⱃⱡl.

II.

ⴹ' αιⱅⱂιⱃ, αιⱂ ⱄ-ⱅⱃⱃ ⱄⱃⱗⱗ, cⱃⱃⱃ ηα ⱃαoⱂ-Ᵽlαċ,
ʒαⱗ Ᵽⱂⱃ ⱃⱃⱗⱗ ȝⱂⱗⱃⱄ ȝⱃⱃ Ⱨαⱃ αη ȝleoⱃⱄ;
ⱄ'ⱃ ȝⱃⱂ ȝαιⱂⱃⱄ ⱪⱗⱃⱄ ⱪⱃⱃⱂ α η-ⱄⱃⱅċαⱃ Ⱨⱃⱃⱃⱡιⱗⱗ,†
ⱄ'ⱃ cⱂⱃ ċαoⱗ Ⱨⱃⱪⱃⱂ ⱅαⱂ ȝαη ⱅⱃⱃⱃoⱃⱃ—
ⱅⱃⱃ Ċαⱂolⱃⱃ loⱗⱗ 'ⱃ α ċαⱪlαċ ȝlⱗⱃⱃⱅα,
ⱄȝ ⱅαⱂⱂαⱃⱗȝ ⱅαⱂ αⱪαⱃⱗ lⱗ cαⱪαⱃⱂ ⱄ'ⱃⱂ ⱃαoⱂαⱄ,
'Ⱶ ⱗⱃ ⱃⱃαιⱅⱣⱃⱄ ⱃⱗ ⱪoⱗⱗ ⱄo ċlαⱗⱗ Lⱃⱅⱗⱂⱃⱃ,
'Ⱶ ⱪⱗⱃⱄ Ⱨoȝα ʒoιⱄⱡl ⱅⱃⱗⱃⱗ ȝαη ⱅlⱃⱃ 'ⱃ αη ⱅⱃⱂⱂ!

III.

Ⱨeαⱃⱄα ⱪⱗⱃⱄ ȝⱂeαⱗⱗ le Ᵽoⱗⱗ αȝ ⱗȝⱃⱃⱪ,
ⱄ'ⱃ ⱅⱃⱃⱗ ⱪⱃⱗⱗ ȝlⱗⱃⱃⱅα αȝ ⱄⱃⱃⱃ αη ċeⱃⱡl;
Ⱪⱗⱃⱄ cαⱗⱅαⱃ α ⱄ-ⱅeαⱃⱃαⱃⱂ, Ⱨα ⱃⱃⱃαⱃⱂ, αȝ ⱃαoⱂ-
Ⱨlαⱃⱅ,
ⱄ'ⱃ ⱅoȝα ⱃlⱃȝe αȝ clⱃⱃⱂ le Ⱨⱃȝαⱃl ⱄ'ⱃⱃ leoȝαⱗ.
Ⱪⱗⱃⱄ ceαllα αȝⱃⱃ ⱃⱃⱄ ȝαη cⱃⱗⱃⱃⱅe αȝ Ⱂαⱂⱃⱃⱅⱃ,
Ⱪⱗⱃⱄ eαⱃⱪαⱃⱂⱅ ⱄⱃα-ⱄoⱃⱗⱗαⱃċ α ⱄ-ⱅeαⱃⱂoⱃll
ⴹⱂⱂeαⱗ:
Ⱪⱗⱃⱄ ⱃcαⱃⱃeαⱄ αȝⱃⱃ ⱃcαⱗⱂⱃαⱄ αιⱂ ċoⱃⱂlⱃⱃⱅ ⱗȝⱃⱂ,
'Ⱶαⱃ ⱃⱃⱪαċ ⱃⱃⱅeαċ ʒαoιⱄⱡl ȝo ⱪⱂⱃⱅ 'ⱗ α ⱄeⱃⱃȝ!

---

* *Donn Firineach,* or *Donn the Truthteller,* to whom is attributed, in Irish mythology, the government of the fairies of Munster. His residence is said to be on Cnock-firinn, a romantic hill in the County Limerick. The *Mangaire Sugach,* the author of this bold appeal in favour of the exiled house of Stuart, describes Donn as bidding him proclaim to the Brave that the hour had arrived for the last glorious effort on behalf of Charles.

Donn is an historical personage, and is said to have been one of

No friend to cheer my visions dreary,
  Save generous Donn, the king of Faëry,
Who mid the festal banquet airy,
  These strains prophetic thus did speak :—

II.

" Behold how chieftains glorious, regal,
  Are bondage-bound, dishonour'd, low ;
These churls from Phelim's heirdom legal,
  And Eiver's lands, are doomed to go ;
For fleets, and Charles brave to lead 'em,
  Will reach our shore with promis'd freedom ;
And vengeance doubly dark shall speed 'em,
  Till bursts their might upon the foe.

III.

" And bards shall pour their tuneful treasure,
  And minstrels strike their voiceful string,
And Tara wake to music's measure,
  And priests be cherish'd by their king ;
And sacred rites and mass-bells sounding
  All Erin's holy domes be found in,
And scattering fear the foe astounding,
  While all the Gael exulting sing.

the sons of Milesius, the celebrated king of Spain. When these
princes invaded Ireland, more than a thousand years before the
Christian Era, Donn, with all his ship's company, was cast away
on the west coast of Munster. It is a curious fact that the name
of this prince, after the lapse of forgotten ages, is as familiar as a
household word among the peasantry of the south !

+ Feidhlim, son of Tuathal Teachtmar, and father of Conn of the
Hundred Battles, was monarch of Ireland at the commencement
of the second century of the Christian Era. It was in the person
of his father, Tuathal Teachtmar, or the Acceptable, that the
Milesian dynasty was restored after the Attacotic rebellion.

IV.

Sιη aʒaτ ó τúr ʒaċ ρún ba ṁéιη lιom,
  2l'r meaṁρκʒ ⱃéιη mo ⱃceól τo ċaċ ;
Τιʒeaτ ʒaċ cρobaιⱃe a ʒ-cobaιη le Séaρlaⱃ,
  Cⱃṁηιʒ aη coηⱃaτ ρéυb aρ ηáṁaιτ—
Sιη aʒaιƀ aη τaη, a'r ʒabaιʒ le ċéιle,
Pⱃeabaιʒ le ⱃoηη a'r pleaηηcaιʒ méιτ-ⱃoιc ;
leaηaιʒ aη ⱃoʒa aιⱃ τρoιηʒ aη éιτιċ,
'S ηá ḣ-ιoⱃρκʒeaτ aéη le ⱃcáτ τ'η η-ʒleóτ !

——:o:——

OL-ⱅ2lN eOʒ2lJN RU2lJḊ UJ SḣUJLLJOBḣ2lJN.

1.

Céaτ rláη ċuⱅ ʒaċ ριʒ-ⱡιⱃ
Bḣeιτeaċ páιⱃⱅeaċ τaⱅ ⱃlιʒⱃe,
2l τ-τιʒ aη ⱅábaιⱃⱃe τo ⱃηṗⱃeaċ,
  le ḣ-íηⱅιη aʒ ól,
ⱅo ⱅρáιʒⱡιoċ ηa ⱡιoηⱅa,
ʒaη ʒⱃáιⱃʒaιⱃ, ʒaη bⱃκʒeaηⱅa,
'Sa ⱅáιⱃeaċ τa τρκⱅ rιη, ;
  Na ʒoιⱡⱡeaċ aιⱃ bⱃóη—
  2lⱅaⱃ ηí ⱅιⱃe aη buc reó
  ⱅo ċⱃuṁτeaⱃ aη τ-óⱃ,
ⱅa baιⱃιuʒaτ ʒo ⱡιoⱃ boċτ,
  2lr τaoιⱃe eιle τá ól !

IV.

" You've heard the secrets I've unfolden;
    To memories true their truths bestow;
And speak, 'twill all the brave embolden,
    The treaty broken by the foe:
But now's the hour—your powers uniting,
    Arise to crush these he-goats blighting;
And while the race of treachery smiting,
    Let none his vengeance wild forego !"

———:o:———

OWEN ROE O'SULLIVAN'S DRINKING SONG.

I.

This cup's flowing measure
I toast to that treasure,
The brave man whose pleasure
        Is quaffing rich wine,
Who deep flagons draining,
From quarrels abstaining,
The morn finds remaining
        All joyous divine—
        It ne'er shall be mine
        To gather vile coin,
To clowns at life's waning,
        For aye to resign !

II.

Bjoɲ báoċlaoċ, le cjɲɲeaċⱬ,
Az ꝼáȝajl cámajr ajn ꞃaojⱬjḃ,
A ꞩ-ⱬjȝ aɲ ⱬábajɲɲe ꞩo ꞃꞃóꝼeaċ
　　le ḣ-jɲⱬjɲ az ól ;
Ar ⱬláⱬ ḃéjꞩ aɲ ḃꞃꞩjɳ úꞩ,
'S ar ꝼaȝɲaċ a ȝ-cꞃjċe,
Ar ꞃȝaꝼꝼaɲ ɲa mjlⱬe,
　　Ȝo cꞃꞃɲɲ ꞩá ȝ-cꞃꞩ ꞃⱬójɲ,
　　Nuajn ꞃjɲꝼeaɲ é ajn bóꞃꞩ,
　　'S ȝaɲ ⱬꞃꞃⱬ ajn a ⱬójɲ,
Bjoɲ a ḃeaɲ ꞃúꞩ ꞩá ċaojɲe,
　　le laojⱬjḃ ȝaɲ cójn—

III.

" Na ⱬꞃáċⱬ ajn ɲa ȝɲjoṁaɲⱬajḃ
Bḣj a b-Paɲjr ɲa Ⱬꞃaoj ꞃojn,
Na'ɲ Jaꞃoɲ ꞩo ꞃjolċajꞩ
　　Ⱬaꞃ ⱬaojꞩ lejr aɲ ꞃeóꞩ ;
Laoċꞃajꞩ ɲa Cꞃaojḃe,
Na'ɲ ⱬe ꞃjɲ ꞩo ċlaojꞩ Ⱬalc,
Na Séaꞃaɲ ċꞃꞃ cjor ajn
　　A ɲ-ꞩjꞃeaċ ȝo leóꞃ,
　　O ! ꞩo ⱬꞃꞃꝼjɲɲꞃj aɲ Aṫójɲ,
　　Ȝaċ cꞃjoċ ejle ꞩe'ɲ ⱬ-ꞃóꞃⱬ,
'Ar ȝaċ acꞃa ḃjꞩ ajȝe,
　　e ⱬaḃajꞃⱬ ċúmꞃa beó ! "

IV.

" Aṫo ċár, jr ⱬú aɲ ꞃȝejṁle,
Ajn ċláꞃaċꞃḃ ꞃjɲⱬe,
Ar ȝo ḃꞃáⱬ béaꞩ aꞩ ċaojɲe,

II.

Some churls will come slinking,
To practise cheap drinking,
Where the generous are linking
    New joys to the old—
Vile starveling ! what matter
If curses should shatter
Your land-marks, and scatter
      To strangers your gold !
      When laid in the mould,
      All naked and cold,
Your dames thus may patter
    Your death-song, behold :—

III.

" Let heroes strike under ;
At Paris why wonder,
Or Jason, who plunder
    From dragons did rive ?
The red-branched hero
May sink down to zero ;
And Cæsar and Nero
    In vain with him strive.
    Let the rich herds arrive
    That in Munster survive,
And I'll yield them, my dear, oh !
    To clasp thee alive !

IV.

" My soul ! how grief's arrow
Hath fix'd in my marrow !
O'er that cold coffin narrow

Ꝺo ꝺτéιẑ aιn mo ẑlón !
Ꝺan laṁaꝺ mo ṙιnⲅean,
S beιτ laιτneaċ le ⲅιne,
Ꝺo b-ⲅeánn lıom anıⲅ τu
    Na mιlτe ꝺe'n ón !
Nι ιoⲅⲅaꝺ mé ⲅeoιꝺ,
    'S nιl ⲅⲏm aẑam a nẑnoꝺ,
' ᴀⲅ nι ⲋáẑⲅaιꝺ me an ċιll
    O mo bⲏꝺneaċ ẑo ꝺeóẑ !"

v.

" ᴀ ċáιnꝺe mo ċⲅoιꝺe 'ⲅτιẑ ;
Cιꝺιẑ láιτneaċ am ⲋιmċιoll,
Nι ⲋáẑⲅaιꝺ me τⲏnτ aιn
    ᴀon τaob ꝺιom ẑan ⲅτⲅóιc !
Nι ⲅτaꝺⲅaꝺ ꝺon τⲅιoẑ ⲅιn,
Ꝺo m-báτan ⲅan laoι me,
'S ẑo bⲅáτ beιτ ꝺá ċaoιne
    ᴀꝺo ċaoιn ⲋean ꝺan nó "—
Ba noιⲙe leaτ ẑaċ ꝺeon
Bⲏéιꝺeaċ anuaⲅ le na ⲅⲅóιn
' ᴀⲅ ι a baẑaιⲅτ ẑo ⲏ·ιⲅeall
    ᴀιn ċⲅιċιꝺ ⲋιn óιẑ !

I'll weep evermore—
By the hand of my father!
This moment I'd rather
From the grave thee to gather,
  Than gold's yellow store !
  All feasts I'll give o'er ;
  I'm stricken and frore—
Oh, grave at Kilmather,
  Be my roof-tree and floor !

v.

" My bosom friends inner,
 Gather round your poor sinner ;
My kerchief and pinner
  To pieces shall go.
In the Lee wildly springing,
I'll end this beginning,
His death-song still singing
  Who valued me so "—
  While round tears thus flow,
  And wailing and woe,
To a youth near her clinging ;
  She beckons alow !

172 *Irish Popular Songs.*

caisiol mumhan.*

I.

Do ġlacfaiṅ ṫú ʒaṅ ba ʒaṅ pṅ́ṅꞇ, ʒaṅ áiṅeaṅ
ꞅṗṅéiö,
A ċṅ̇ö öö'ṅ ꞇ-ꞅaoiʒil le ꞇoil öo ṁṅ̇ṅꞇiṅ öa m'áill
ṅeaꞇ mé ;
Sé mo ġalaṅ öuaċ ʒaṅ mé 'ʒuꞅ ꞇú, a öioṅ ʒṅáö
mo ċléiḃ,
A ʒ-Caiṅiol Múṁaṅ, aꞅ ʒaṅ öo leabaiö ꝼṅ́ṅ aċ aṅ
cláṅ buʒ öéal !

II.

Siúḃail a ċoʒaṅ 'aꞅ ꞇaṅṅ a ċoöla liom ꝼéiṅ öö'ṅ
ʒleaṅṅ,
Ġeabaiö ꞇú ꝼoꞅʒaö leabaiö ꝼlocuiꞅ aʒuꞅ aöaṅ coiꞅ
aṁaṅ ;
Béiö ṅa ꞅṅoꞇa a ʒaḃájal ṫṅaiṅ̃, ꝼaoi ʒéuʒaiḃ
cṅaṅṅ,
Béiö aṅ loṅ öuḃ ṅ'aṅ b-ꝼocaiṅ, 'ꞅaṅ ċiaṅꞅaċ áṅṅ.

III.

Seaṅc mo ċléiḃ öo ṫuʒ mé ꝼéiṅ öṅꞇ, a'ꞅ ʒṅáö
ꞇṅe ṅúṅ,
Da ö-ꞇiʒꝼeaö ꞅé öo ċoṅ 'ꞅa ꞇ-ꞅaoʒal ʒo m-béiöiṅ
ꝼéiṅ a'ꞅ ꞇú,

* *Caisiol Mumhan, Cashel of Munster,* is the most popular of
all the Irish melodies. This will perhaps account for the reason
that there is no Irish song of which there are so many corrupt versions as this. I cannot undertake to say that the present is the

CASHEL OF MUNSTER.

I.

I would wed you, dear, without gold or gear, or
counted kine ;
My wealth you'll be, would your friends agree, and
you be mine—
My grief, my gloom! that you do not come, my
heart's dear hoard !
To Cashel fair, though our couch were there but a
soft deal board !

II.

Oh, come, my bride, o'er the wild hills' side, to the
valley low,
A downy bed, for my love I'll spread, where waters
flow ;
And we shall stray, where streamlets play, the groves
among,
Where echo tells, to the listening dells, the blackbird's
song !

III.

Love, tender, true I gave to you, and secret sighs,
In hope to see, upon you and me, one hour arise,

genuine one, but in its simple pathos it bears strong evidence of
authenticity. It was given me by a lady of the County Clare,
whose mother, she informed me, was accustomed to sing it, at the
advanced age of eighty years.

Ceaṅȝal cléıṗeaċ eaⱱṗỹ aṗaoṅ, 'ṛ aṅ ḟáıṅṅe
ⱱluċ ;

Ꝺ'ṛ ⱱá bḟeıcḟỹ ḟéıṅ mo ṫeaṗc aȝ aoṅ ḟeaṗ ȝeıⱱỹ
báṛ le cúṁaıⱱ !

IV.

Ꝺıa-ⱱoṁṅȝċ, 'ṅuaıṛ a ċjóıṅṅ aȝ aṅ Ⱬeampoll í,
Ḟallȝṅṅ ṛıaṁaċ a'ṛ ṅıbíṅ uaıṫṅe ṅṛṛe aṅuṅ maṛ
ȝṅaoı ;

Ꝺȝuṛ ȝúaṅa ⱱo ṛȝuabḟaⱱ ṅa ȝleaṅṅⱫa ḟṛaoıċ :
Oċ ! ṛé mo buaıṗeaⱱ maṛ ⱱo luaⱱeaⱱ lıom ṅa
maıȝⱱeañ í !

V.

Ⱬa úṛ pıob aȝ mo ṁṛṛṅíṅ, 'ṛ a bṛáȝaıⱱ maṛ aol,
Ꝺ cṅíjṅ caṛⱱa buacalaċ aȝ ḟáṛ ȝo ḟéuṛ ;
Sé mo ċuṁa ṅıṁe ṅaċ ṛaṅ ṅṛ ṫíoṛ ⱱo ḟáȝaⱱ me
Ⱬaṛ a ṛⱫıṛṅıȝeaⱱ mé a ȝ-cóıȝıb a'ṛ mo ȝṗáⱱ ċaṛ
m'ⱱéıṛ !

Cṛíoċ.

When the priest's blest voice would confirm my
  choice, and the ring's strict tie :
If wife you be, love, to one but me, love, in grief
  I'll die !

IV.

In church at pray'r first I saw the fair in glorious
  sheen,
In mantle flowing, with jewels glowing, and frontlet
  green,
And robe of whiteness, whose fold of lightness might
  sweep the lea ;
Oh, my heart is broken since tongues have spoken
  that maid for me !

V.

A neck of white has my heart's delight, and breast
  like snow,
And flowing hair, whose ringlets fair to the green
  grass flow—
Alas ! that I did not early die, before the day
That saw me here, from my bosom's dear, far, far
  away !

THE END.

LIBRARY
17 AUG
UNIVERSITY OF TORONTO

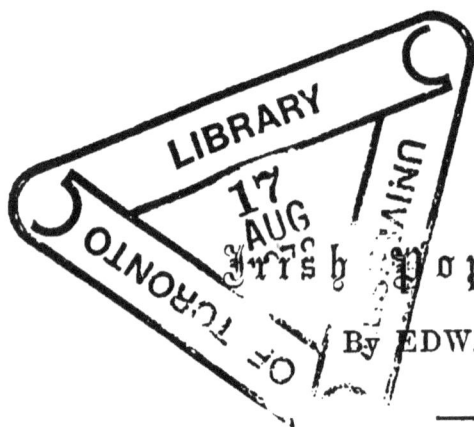

Irish Popular Songs.

By EDWARD WALSH.

——:o:——

Press Notices of the First Edition—1847.

From the " Dublin Warder."

" This little volume is dedicated to the people of Ireland, by one
who has given a great portion of his time and attention to the
examination and illustration of their metrical literature. . . . . .
Mr. Walsh has done a service to our national language by his
metrical translations, in which we feel quite confident the spirit of
the original is preserved as the measure is, so as to emit the 'song-
tune' of the Irish ballad. The little volume is brought out in an
attractive dress, at a low price, and must prove an accession to our
national literary collection."

From the " Dublin Weekly Register."

" The translator of these songs has brought to his task a
thoroughly competent knowledge and appreciation of the Irish
language, considerable practice and aptitude for translation, and
poetic feeling. Mr. Walsh has done in this instance, what should
be done in all cases where the pieces are numerous enough to fill a
separate publication, given the translation on the one page, the
original on the opposite. The style of the rendering is free,
smooth, and pleasing, and not unfrequently at once vigorous and
harmonious."